E4C

DISORDER PRESS
New Orleans & Somewhere Else in America
disorderpress.com

E4C

EXCHANGE FOR CHANGE
Miami, FL
exchange-for-change.org

–

COVER & BOOK DESIGN
Michelle Nazzal

FRONT COVER ILLUSTRATIONS
Kevin M. Moore

BACK COVER ILLUSTRATION
William Smith

BACK COVER QUOTE
Zaza Rivera

–

All pieces in this anthology were collected
and written in 2020.

ISBN: 978-0-9975766-5-8

First Edition – June 2021
Printed & Bound in Pennsylvania

HEAR US

WRITING FROM THE INSIDE
DURING THE TIME OF COVID

Foreword by
Edwidge Danticat

Today is June 29. So far one man has tested positive in this dorm. He was removed this morning, and an official has just come to notify us we are on lockdown quarantine.

ERIC FINLEY

COVID-19 HAS INVADED OUR WORLD, AND INVISIBLE KILLER OUTSIDE OF OUR MASK. I REALLY DON'T KNOW IF SOCIETY SHOULD BLAME IT ON A INCOMPINTENT TRUMP ADMINISTRATION, WHO FROM MY ACCESSMENT OF REALITY SEEM'S TO BE TRYING TO MAKE A POPULATION ADJUSTMENT AT THE COST OF U.S. CITIZEN'S LIVES.

RODERICK RICHARDSON

AS A TORRENT OF DOUBT FLOODS A RIVER OF TEARS,

AND A SUFFERING DREAD CRIPPLES WORRY-WRACKED MINDS,

SILVER LININGS REACH OUT, WELL-ENTRENCHED AGAINST FEAR,

AND HOLD FAST TO A PLEDGE TO HELP MAN THE FRONTLINE.

AMID PLEAS FOR A PEACE FROM WHAT'S TAKEN ITS TOLL,

AMONG ALL WHO ARE TRAPPED IN A MOUNTAIN OF LOSS,

SILVER LININGS RELEASE, FROM THE DEPTHS OF THEIR SOULS,

THE RAW COURAGE THEY'VE TAPPED IN SUPPORT OF THE CAUSE.

SEAMUS FENWAY

We will see how tuff you are
Once you are behind bars

HOWARD OVERTURF

NOTES FROM OUR TEAM

Having a small press gives us a platform to lift voices that often go unheard. With this platform comes responsibility. During the pandemic and the aftermath of George Floyd's murder, we had a lot of time to contemplate what kind of book we wanted to publish next. We were blessed to be introduced to the people at Exchange for Change. Without their guidance we would never have been exposed to such incredible writing from the inside and those whose lives have been touched by mass incarceration. We are honored to publish the work of these individuals.

Exchange for Change, a South Florida-based nonprofit that teaches writing in federal and Florida prisons — as well as juvenile residential centers — was looking for the perfect partner for this book project. Disorder Press complements our mission to provide communication and writing skills to the incarcerated population and bring their voices to the outside world.

→

CONTENTS

SECTION II

SECTION III

SECTION IV

INDEX

→

FOREWORD

"Do you understand what it means when you have absolutely nowhere to turn?" Semyon Zakharovich Marmeladov, an out of favor, and out of luck father asks in Dostoevsky's 19th century novel, *Crime and Punishment*. In *Hear Us, Writing from the Inside During the Time of COVID*, a collection of essays, poems, sketches, drawings, and other types of writing and artwork, these contributors pose a similar question of themselves and of us, their readers, during the time of COVID-19.

While so many of us are dreaming of a post-COVID future and all the things we'd like to do once the specter of the coronavirus has been lifted, for many of these incarcerated writers and artists, and their family members, the future will likely proceed much like the past, except with increased urgency. The confinement, or quarantine, we are all so eager to dodge, the creators in this book experience every day. Many of them know all too well what it's like to be placed in isolation, while also being unable to find ways to self-isolate when they need to.

"Personal space is a luxury of the free world," Lance E. Palermo writes in his piece, "Social Deprivation." "If you ask any inmate when social distancing began, they'll probably say the first day of their incarceration," Eduardo Martinez concurs in "COVID Crazy." "Nevertheless, the whole country has become a prison and who better to speak on that than a prisoner."

Those who have worked with our contributors "on the inside," like the teachers and supporters of Exchange for Change, the Miami-based organization publishing this book with Disorder Press, do not ask them why they are incarcerated. This seems like the last bit of space not invaded and is the incarcerated person's story to tell. It goes without saying that no act described or not described here is being condoned, nor is any point of view being endorsed, by the publication of these words. For my part, I took heed to the call of the title, ("Hear Us") and I listened, which is what I hope you, the reader, will do as well.

Just as we wouldn't be aware of certain heinous crimes resulting from police and vigilante murders if there were no recordings of them, we cannot turn away from the voices here, as they document this moment and time, both in their acceptance and their denial of the virus, their theories about its sources, their lightheartedness and seriousness, their outcry and their pain. We must also listen to family members writing "from the outside," family members like Tina Barrett who, in "Untitled," writes of her incarcerated brother's death from COVID-19, "I feel certain no one will care about the person I lost because he was in prison."

There are moments of levity in these pages as well. Some of our contributors find irony and humor in unexpected places. In "Throw Away the Keys Please," Dave Becker writes, "Prison, for all intents and purposes, has finally become an agreeable location to wait out the storm...My aunt told me how she almost came to blows with another lady in the grocery store because the other lady wasn't wearing a mask and she was creeping up on my aunt (who has lung issues). I haven't had a good fight story to tell in months."

Writing about the menace of COVID-19 on death row, Bob R. (Cowboy) Williams Jr. observes in his elegiac piece listing the names of friends lost to COVID-19 — "In Memoriam: 2020's COVID-19 Losses to the Death Row Community" — "(T)he cold hard fact, at least for me, is that they are going to kill me one day...And then, something comes along, something we can't really even square up to and fight."

Many of our contributors have lost friends on the inside as well as family members on the outside, and not just to the coronavirus. The 2020 killings of, among others, Ahmaud Arbery, Breonna Taylor, and the over nine-minute long knee-to-neck suffocation of George Floyd by Derek Chauvin, led to writing and art that felt as though their creators were trying to encourage victims of vigilante and police murders, as well as those dying from the coronavirus, to breathe.

In "I Can't Breathe," Helena L Payne writes,

I demand to stand on my feet
And be treated like a human being
Don't take my life away from me

In "A Breathing Tribute," Pierre Pinsen writes, "I had been in George Floyd's position a number of times before I was the age of 15. I thought that a knee on my back was standard operating procedure, that I was born to supply the neck as a resting place for oppression...COVID-19 has helped many of these Black men recognize their vulnerability. Police brutality has helped to reveal that they are endangered."

As I write these words, in a rare conviction of a police officer, Derek Chauvin has just been found guilty of second and third-degree murder, and second-degree manslaughter, for the killing of George Floyd. Minutes before the verdict was read, a 15-year-old Black girl, Ma'Khia Bryant, was shot and killed by the police in Columbus, Ohio. A few days before, Daunte Wright, a 20-year-old, was shot and killed by the police a few miles from where Chauvin's trial was being held. A few weeks before that, a police officer fatally shot a 13-year-old boy, Adam Toledo, in Chicago as he held both his hands up in the air.

As Derek Chauvin himself enters the carceral state, to live "on the inside" and as other Black and Brown people continue to die from both police violence and the corona-virus — these words from Ms. Alisha Michelle Ward's poem, "Untitled," come to mind:

Floyd's tragedy would've been another blip in our minds
If the virus hadn't given us so much idle time.
First we were appalled, then we were sad,
Unconsoled in our grief, and then we got mad.
A movement was born with a legitimate cause

I think, too, of these lines from James Terry II's piece, "Harlem World,"

Seek and you shall find oppressed voices reaching out to
be heard.

Edwidge Danticat

EDUARDO MARTINEZ

"

QUARANTINE IS A WORD THAT EVERY INMATE NOW KNOWS HOW TO SPELL

"

THE SHAKEDOWN

LESMES CASERES

Today in South Bay Correctional
Prisoners look at prison staff with a side eye.
The convict wonders which staff member could kill him.
A teacher turned nurse barges into our home.
He wears a mask.
He barks orders.
He aims a gun, a thermometer, at the head of a gangster.
No smile.
He squeezes the trigger.
He takes...our temperature.
An accomplice does the numbers.
Another guards the door.
I keep my distance.
I do as they say.
Please, I silently pray, I have a kid at home! I don't
want to die in here!
They herd us into our cages and lock us in.
Time to count.
I count.
I count the bricks and fall into a dream.
Of a line for rations of food,
Of a sinister king who laughs and rubs his round belly,
Of birds, white and blue.
I'm on a turbulent plane.
I dash to the cockpit and find it empty.
I'm in China, where I walk the Great Wall.
Count clears.
I wash my hands and heart of fear.

COVID CRAZY

EDUARDO MARTINEZ

If you ask any inmate when social distancing began,
they'll probably say the first day of their incarceration. That's right around the same time society started
viewing inmates as viruses. Being sick and tired of
being sick and tired was already the daily mentality
before the pandemic began. When Corona first hit the U.S.
we took it in stride. Even went through the ridiculous
toilet tissue frenzy, never really thinking we'd be dealing with this ten months later (toilet paper was never
that important huh?). Nevertheless, the whole country has
become a prison and who better to speak on that than
a prisoner.

My view of the world comes from a television that feeds
us society on a plastic spoon. And my perspective is a
good cold one, like leftover pizza. I don't agree with
a lot of misleading information the media puts out.
And if you've been in prison you'd understand why. I've
learned to question everything. Like Alex Trebek, my
mind is never satisfied with a simple yes or no. I know
that whether you're left-wing or right-wing you're still
part of the same bird, and being liberal is just letting
the bird out of the cage. Because to me this virus has
become political, so it wouldn't surprise me if the virus
disappeared after the presidential election, and hopefully it does.

Would it surprise you if you were told that Medicaid pays
every hospital an average of 13,000 dollars for every
patient they stamp with Corona, and between 40,000 to
60,000 for every one that is on a respirator? So when the
positive test results rise and the people panic, forgive me if I don't ring the alarm. Is this a crisis? It

absolutely is. Even though the hidden agenda might
be monetary and political, the fact remains that people
are dying.

I've grown weary of acronyms, like W.H.O, C.D.C, A.L.E.C,
and D.O.C. Just like I won't trust the vaccine. I expect
it to be mandated, like wearing masks and social distancing. But if it's something I can keep out of my system while living stuck inside this system, that's what I
plan to do.

I lost my sense of smell and taste months ago, along
with everyone else in my dorm. This is not a bad thing if
you've ever eaten prison food or have been confined and
clustered with over 82 men in a Florida prison dormitory
with no A.C. or proper ventilation.

Survival is a key ingredient in here, so I made it over
the hurdles, but the marathon continues. We were quarantined (quarantine is a word that every inmate now
knows how to spell) for 71 days in my housing area.
Aggressions, frustration, depression, oppression, and
everything else that rhymes negatively with those words
were feelings that were passed around like a joint in
this South Florida heat.

Because it seemed like the more that people protested
and fell ill out there, the more oppressive our situations became. I went weeks without feeling the sun on
my skin; my body was thirsty for some sunny delight. But
if you want a sense of what power is, it's being able to
control the sun. Because if they don't want you to see
the sun, you won't. How powerful is that?

I haven't seen my family since February, 2020. So it
tickles me stupid when I hear the complaints of people
being temporarily stuck in the luxuries of their home
and among family. Six feet of separation would be a warm

embrace to me if I was at home with my people. But it seems like everyone is more concerned about themselves and not their neighbors (especially if those neighbors are incarcerated). I'm trying my best to remain positive, minus a Q-tip up my nose, with all the sickness and death that's plaguing our humanity. Because I just want to be down to earth without ending up six feet deep, no matter how sick and tired this country gets.

ARTWORK BY: ANONYMOUS, INCARCERATED IN
THE STATE OF FLORIDA

UNTITLED

TINA BARRETT

The media is full of stories about the wonderful people being lost to this pandemic. I have feelings of ambivalence for these reports. On the one hand the touching tributes most certainly hit the heartstrings of many. You can almost hear "Such a loss..." echoing back from the multitudes as we all imagine what a great person they were and how terrible it is that he or she is no longer with us, such a loss. On the other hand I feel certain no one will care about the person I lost because he was in prison. I've considered writing a touching tribute so that his name and his story could be heard and my pain could be shared, even if only for a minute or two, but then I pause.

It would not be difficult to do. My brother was a wonderful human being and I do not use any of those words lightly or without insight. This is not grief remembering only the good and filtering out the bad. My brother was a wonderful human being. He started off that way, and he ended that way though, as with all of us, there were many ups and downs along his path. I can still see him sitting in his highchair smushing mashed potatoes into his hair and packing them down very carefully. My mother insisted that his hair stood up on its ends because of this practice. I was careful to keep mashed potatoes out of my own hair for this very reason. He was a cute kid and I loved him even though he was two years younger and got me in trouble with some frequency for the messes he would make.

I remember when he was 16 he single-handedly dug a hole for a septic tank big enough for a four-bedroom house through solid limestone because our family could not afford to have a back-hoe digger come out and

spend the ten minutes it would take. He did not complain, he just did it because he was the only one of us
physically capable of the job and we needed him to do
it. Two years later, while I was in college and needing help with my rent, John volunteered to send me an
allotment every month from his Army salary so I could
stay in school. He was 18 and he paid my rent of his
own volition because he was able to do so and I needed
him. He was a good kid and I loved him even though I
often criticized his taste in music and clothing. He
was hardworking and generous even as a very young man.

There are many, many more stories of how my brother rose
to the occasion to help the people he loved when they
needed him. Only after his passing did I learn of the
many people I didn't know who had similar stories of "JB"
and his commitment and generosity of spirit to those in
need of him and his abilities. He was a good man and even
though he was in prison, there are no caveats to that
statement. He was a good man and he will be missed.

But the reality is that my brother's incarceration, for the
general public, makes his passing less painful somehow. He
was "just a prisoner" I suppose they might say. How can I
convince them otherwise? I am biased, we can all see that.
But there are sound reasons for why the loss of someone
like my brother is to be felt as heavily as any other.

As a Christian I would invoke the words of the King
James Bible my grandmother carried: "Verily I say unto
you, Inasmuch as ye have done it unto one of the least
of these my brethren, ye have done it unto me," (Matthew
25:40). If you are not inclined to think of prisoners as

having much, if any, value in our society, then you must consider them to be 'the least' and Jesus would have you realize that as much as you would do for him you should do for them. If we as a society cannot offer those we imprison basic needs, then we Christians would seem to be living in a society that does not live up to what we profess to be. My brother died in a hospital after suffering for an unknown period of time. He was shuttled about in his final days. He was admitted to the hospital in which he died to have 'ulcer surgery.' No one was paying attention to what he needed, they were playing hot potato with him because he died of COVID-19 two days later. They passed him, and responsibility for him, around until he died. I do not believe this is how we should treat anyone, even 'the least' of our people.

But I'm not a prisoner, and the reality is that the manner in which my brother was treated impacts me as well. I only learned he was sick and he died because the hospital called me. His final words must have been to tell them how to reach us because the Department of Corrections has yet to send us anything to explain his death or even that he died. I'd have taken responsibility for him if offered the chance. We were allowed to agree to take him off of life support; that was all the input we were offered.

The indignities do not end there. If you have ever lost a loved one, you know that their belongings, no matter how simple, can mean a great deal. I have a jelly glass in my cupboard that my grandfather drank from every day when he took his medicine. It is just a silly little glass with a *Tom and Jerry* cartoon printed on the side but it is precious to me. The prison has sent me nothing that belonged to my brother and I know he had belongings because I had to buy them from the approved vendors at the approved times. I don't know where any of them are or if I will ever see the things he kept close and safe all those years. The only thing I have of my brother's are his ashes and I paid for those also. If you cannot muster compassion for 'the least' of our people in prison, perhaps you can put yourself in the place of a sister or a mother or a child who has a loved one in jail or prison. Simple empathy should be enough to appreciate why we as a society should care about our prisoners no matter what they did or did not do to get themselves in prison.

If you cannot find it in yourself to have sympathy for prisoners as 'the least' of our people, or empathy for those of us who love them, perhaps the reality that people get out of prison either better or worse than they went in, and that that also has an impact on all of us, is enough to realize that we should all care about what happens to inmates. My brother all but ran the Education Department of a large Florida prison. He was not on the payroll and had no retirement assets to pass on to his heirs, but he taught music to many and life lessons to all who would take the time to listen. He was funny, articulate, intelligent and persuasive. He influenced the lives of many, always for the better, and that includes fellow inmates, volunteers and employees. His words, his deeds, and his example are carried by many in and out of incarceration.

When he died he did not merely leave a gaping hole in the world in which he lived and worked. He left a hole that is unlikely to be filled. When most of us die we are mourned but there are people waiting in the wings to fill our shoes. That is not the case with my brother. No one aspires to go to prison and devote their lives and their time to helping others improve themselves and serve as an example to the need to make better decisions when they leave. There are no bright, enthusiastic, young people ready to pick up where he left off. He gave much but his giving is over; there will be no more recipients of his insights and his wisdom. He had much to give and like it or not, we all lose when someone like my brother stops giving. Men will continue to go into prisons and leave prisons but JB's ability to impact their lives is done. My little brother, John C. Barrett, died at the age of 55 from COVID-19. He was a good man and a fine teacher. He will be missed by many who loved him and who will mourn him, but he will also be missed, albeit unknowingly, by many that could have benefitted from having known him. His death is a loss to his family, to his friends and to this society. I care because I was his sister, but everyone should care because we really are all in this together.

TESTED

MUHAMMAD ABDULMALIK AL-HANAFI

[Personal Journal Entry: 12 May 2020]

I tested positive for COVID-19. I find this challenging
for several reasons:

1) I am not convinced that I have it. I was probably
exposed to it; the first confirmed case was, after all,
someone I associated with regularly. However, he was
evacuated 18 days before I was tested, and he claimed he
had been experiencing symptoms for four days prior to
that. Whether we count it 18 or 22 days, I was well over
14 days from exposure and I never experienced a symptom
that I could unequivocally associate with COVID-19.

Furthermore, I have been a practicing Orthodox Sunni
Muslim ever since 16 Ramadan (18 September) 2008. I was
tested on 6 May this year, which was also 13 Ramadan.
During my exposure, I have been in a weakened state due
to fasting. Nevertheless, I cannot report any symptoms
that would not normally be associated with fasting.

In addition, I was dedicated to social distancing, hand
sanitizing and washing, and my cloth face masks, each
one customized with an abjurative verse from the Qur'an.
When I was tested, it was a mass test with a hundred-plus
samples. There is a chance that my sample could have been
confused with a positive sample, and I cannot get retested.

2) The quarantine procedures implemented at this institution are hazardous. They have segregated everyone who
"tested positive" into one unit, with cellmates, and
locked the unit down. This will guarantee that everyone in the unit is exposed to the virus. If I do have it,
I have been fighting it for at least eight days, and if

someone else is quarantined with me who has only been battling for four, then by the time I am "clear," he could re-expose me to it.

3) I wonder how this will affect mass incarceration. The institution is already starting to take disciplinary action against prisoners who do not comply with the quarantine demands. Tennessee Department of Corrections (TDOC) does this in the form of written sanctions which go into a prisoner's institutional file. The parole board reviews this file to determine a prisoner's "rehabilitative progress." Now, in addition to the other arbitrary prohibitions which contribute to mass incarceration and overcrowding (such as cell phones and tobacco, which are not against the law, yet are sanctioned with prison time via parole boards and institutional disciplinary procedures), we also have violations related to COVID-19.

4) Moreover, as ironic as it is testing, I have made it sixteen years in some of Tennessee's worst prisons, and now I may die from a virus engineered by the Chinese government to exterminate their Muslim population (which the whole world seems to have forgotten about; or at least completely stopped talking about). The anti-Muslim germ escaped China, came all the way to America, and may now kill me. Nevertheless, nothing can happen unless it is G-d's will, we put our trust in Him, and unto Him we all return.

[Four Months Later, Entry: 11 September 2020]

I have not been able to call my mother. She has asthma and chronic bronchitis. She is also weak, due to the western kufaar drug dealers, who push intoxicants under the pseudonym "prescription medication." As the Messenger foretold that in the end times, people would presume to make intoxicants okay by referring to them with other names. She lives with my sister, Rydia. Rydia is also weak, psychologically due to mental illnesses and physically due to her prescriptions, which includes the extra substances that the kufaar require her to take for the purpose of "transitioning" her appearance from male to female. Rydia is also addicted to non-prescription drugs, and she will not abide by the quarantine.

Throughout my incarceration, I have been tested by speculation over potential threats to my family. When hurricanes travel all the way to New York; when terrorists and mass-shooters make the headlines; when police brutality is more public than ever, and peaceful protests burgeon into civil unrest; and now, when the whole world is at the mercy of...whom? G-d is the Supreme Arbitrator of the entire universe, notwithstanding; to what part of the universe do we look to cast blame? Whom do we unleash our vengeance upon for this worldwide decimation? What prevents us from avenging the slaughtered but cowardice? My mother and sister are not Muslim, yet the Chinese weapon threatens to wipe them out as surely as my brothers and sisters in the Chinese camps, as surely as the poor in American prisons, and as surely as everyone else in the world. G-d demands justice from mankind. Where is all of the might of the American imperialist war machine, while communists casually exterminate the human race? When the world actually needs us to intervene, why do we not fight? Will we only bully weaker nations, when true threats to liberty persist through world powers? No country on Earth could withstand the full force of the United States, head on, not even China. Why are we content to simply prepare for war? Why not use our power to answer oppression with justice? Where is all of the fanatical fervor of the Wahabi terrorist network? You slaughter innocents by the thousands, because you are impoverished, ignorant, and bored! You slaughter Muslims! You claim to justify your wanton bloodlust by citing the Book of G-d, and now Muslims are being exterminated...and you HIDE! You have surrendered to the friends of Satan and turned your backs when faced with a legitimate call to jihad!

I am not on this planet exclusively as a Muslim. I live
with non-Muslims. I was born to a non-Muslim. I am also
an American. As an American Muslim, I wish there was a
way I could lead the world to freedom. I wish I could
inspire them by the Book of G-d, the Qur'an Al Kareem,
the way I am inspired. We should liberate the Chinese
people. We all have a duty, for the survival of life on
this planet, to answer the call for jihad against these
communist kufaar. It is as surely a universal imperative
as the call to Islam itself. Let those who sell the life
of this world for the Hereafter, fight in the Cause
of G-d...

What is wrong with you that you fight not in the Cause
of G-d, and for those weak, ill-treated and oppressed
among men, women, and children, whose cry is: "Our Lord!
Rescue us from this place whose people are oppres-
sors; and raise for us from You one who will protect,
and raise for us from You one who will help." (Qur'an
4:74, 75) Permission to fight is given to those who are
fought against...Those who have been expelled from their
homes unjustly only because they said: "Our Lord is G-d.
For had it not been that G-d checks one set of people
by means of another, monasteries, churches, synagogues
and mosques, wherein the Name of G-d is mentioned much,
would surely have been pulled down. Verily, G-d will help
those who help His Cause. Truly, G-d is All Strong, All-
Mighty." (Q 22:39-40)

If it had been G-d's Will, He Himself could certainly
have punished them. But in order to test some of you by
means of others, (Q47:4) G-d is testing us. How long will
we take to answer His demand for jihad?

I WISH I COULD DURING COVID-19

VICTOR GOMEZ

As a correctional advisor, I wish I could do more for my students. Every day in the United States, the news now states that we are closer to 130,000 human deaths. One human life is enough, but 130,000?! Thousands of our incarcerated students have been affected by the COVID-19 virus. No one seems to care. Prisoners remain locked up with very little help. You can almost feel the tension in the air.

I pray that their family members do not become positive with the COVID-19 virus. I pray that the children of the incarcerated will continue to remain safe and hopefully one day be reunited with their loved ones.

It is sad to not be able to hold your loved one's hand while they are in the hospital, alone, and you are locked up. I wish I could do more, yet my hands are tied due to this virus. I wish I could provide more masks. I wish I did not have to worry so much for my students. I wish I did not have to love so much.

**PERSONAL
SPACE
IS A
LUXURY
OF
THE
FREE
WORLD**

→

WHO'S NEXT

JAMES SOTO

Older prisons have an open-bar construction which makes separation impossible. I sat in my cell watching news reports as the number of positive cases grew. By mid-March, the death toll rose and not excluded was Stateville, which became a "hot spot." I recall hearing fellow prisoners yell for a "med-tech" or a "C-O" (correctional officer) to come to their cell because someone needed medical help. It seemed that with each passing day, the yells were frequently heard echoing throughout the cellhouse, followed by people being wheeled out. Soon, the gallery chatter turned to "who's next" and now those words haunt my psyche.

Days passed by very slowly. I felt so vulnerable. Every sneeze, cough, or stomachache turned into a serious matter — could it be COVID-19? This is no way for anyone to live. Life before the pandemic feels so distant. When it was reported in China, I, along with most people, did not foresee it coming to America. Now that it's here, it reminds me of a sci-fi movie like *Outbreak* or *Contagion*.

People I knew had died and the reality was unavoidable. We were given paper masks and told to wash our hands and living areas often. But no matter the protective measures, the late-night yells continued and people left — some never to return. In time, the National Guard arrived and set up pressurized tents in the gym to hold those who became ill and tested positive. The soldiers, dressed from head-to-toe in PPEs, took our temperatures and heart rates to gauge our oxygen levels. It gave me a sense of relief, but I knew a fever was not the only symptom of COVID-19.

I think that this virus has been around since the beginning of the year. I had a strange illness early on with COVID-like symptoms, but I was told it was just a "stomach bug" and that it would pass. I can't help but wonder if it was this virus. In our society, the homeless, the elderly, the incarcerated, and other marginalized people, are simply ignored and do not receive quality healthcare. I do not wish to say that no help is available, because here they are trying their best, but of course there is room for improvement. When the number of COVID-19 cases spiked, hospitals announced that they did not want to accept any prisoners because of a shortage of bed space and/or ventilators.

I realize that prisons are not meant to be places of comfort or required to provide the best of care. It suffices if they provide "adequate" healthcare, which is interpreted as minimal care. Somehow, humanity is lost in this translation.

PANDEMIC

SAMUEL M. KING

Invisible-stealthy-deadly
Hovering-scary and sinister
The Menace administers
The Reaper's intentions
To deploy the matrix
Of Triple Six (666);
This antisocial virus
Demands social distancing
By six or sick the inevitable
To be carried by six
And ceremoniously deep sixed.

Wearing the protective mask
That unites and divides
The steps are test — treat —
And trace to chase the pest
Out of every place, while
Closing restaurants and malls
Airlines-stores-bingo halls.
Paranoid eyes are downcast
The schools have empty halls
And in the cathedral
Last few Sundays — no mass;
Forced and sequestered
Invaded into isolation

Communication via Zoom
The sinister menace looms,
Residences where the COVID-19
Conspire to preside, are willed
To be exorcised by Chlorides.
The New Aerosol science,
And face mask compliance

Request of patients as victims
To unite by seeking distance
With disinfectants and protectants;
And a can of Lysol stands tall,
As humanity's ally with promise
To attack viruses of sinister coughs.

All the non-essentials
Have lost productive potential,
So many separated and alone
The paradox of separateness
And yet togetherness, while
Tragedy is the news theme,
The ultimate threat to wellness
Purveys a dramatic scene
As futures are cancelled
No vaccines — no antibodies
Experts without answers

Pandemonium too, is spreading
Only God knows where we're heading.
Misinformation — disinformation
Intimidates — dominates and demand
That human beings surrender
Their dreams — goals and plans.
Cognizance of stages and phases
Are colored; red-orange-yellow
Until green, distance is furthered
Corona is a temporary onus.
The song we now sing
I sing in unison and for everyone
We will overcome — only together
Pandemics do not last forever.

PANDEMIC

Invisible - stealthy - deadly
Hovering - scarry and sinister
The Menuce administers
The Reaper's intentions
To deploy the matrix
of Triple six (666);
This anti-social virus
Demands social distancing
by six or risk the inevitable
to be carried by six
11 And ceremoniously deep sixed.

Wearing the protective mask
That unites and divides
The steps are test-treat
and trace to chase the pest
out of every place, while
closing restaurants and malls
Airlines - stores - bingo halls.
   Paranoid eyes are down cast
The schools have empty halls
And in the cathedral
Last few Sundays - no mass;
forced and sequestered
13 Invaded into isolation

Communicating via zoom
The sinister menace looms,
Residences where the covid
Conspire to preside, are willed
To be exorcized by cholorides.
    The New Aerosol science,
And face mask compliance
Request of patients as victims
to unite by seeking distance
with dis-infectants as protectants;
And a can of Lysol stands tall,
as Humanity's ally with promise
13 To attack viruses of sinister coughs.

All the non-essentials
Have lost productive potential,
so many separated and alone
The paradox of separateness
And yet togetherness, while
Tragedy is the news theme,
The ultimate threat to wellness
Purveys a dramatic scene.
As futures are cancelled
No vaccines - No antibodies
11 Experts without answers

UNTITLED

XERXES

The unique experience going on inside my prison related to COVID-19 is the fickle response: testing, mandatory social distancing, mask wearing, and tracing. The Michigan Department of Corrections (MDC) is just now mandating its employees to take COVID-19 tests, six months after the pandemic compelled stay-at-home orders and disrupted normal operations inside correctional facilities. I presume mandatory staff testing is now required because the MDC leads the nation in infection rates.

Despite nearly 4,000 positive tests and 69 deaths, the MDC continues to cross-pollinate the disease with transfers of inmates from facilities with infected prisoners and staff. It is not callous, recklessness, or ignorance driving decision making — it is putting profits over people that is causing Department leaders to compromise the governor's orders and recommendations. Profit over people is the same motivation that drove the Flint Michigan Water Crisis.

The MDC is set up to solicit revenue from the state budget. The state government solicits revenue from state taxpayers and the federal government through its representation of institutional programming like Re-entry, Vocation Trades, and Higher Education. Hence, at the expense of safety precautions, 38,000 prisoners' lives are being jeopardized for operational revenue. The jeopardy is the constant transfer of other prisoners from hot spots to facilities like mine — that had zero positive cases as of June 8, 2020 — to enroll in programs. The more prisoners enrolled in programs, the more revenue siphoned from state, federal, and private budgets.

What's more unique — giving cause to take a deep breath — is the fact that transfers coming from Lakeland Correctional Facility tested positive, battled the virus, and have been integrated into the general population without a COVID-19 test upon arrival or a 14-day quarantine. Prisoners' transfers, inadequate testing upon arrival, and the failure to require mandatory testing of DOC employees for six months — employees who are obviously the carriers as they are the only persons who have been permitted into its correctional facilities since March 11, 2020 — is arguably the reason why the MDC is leading the nation in infection rates.

This pandemic and the collateral damage viewed through a pair of humane lenses should teach us economic equality, political humility, and hospitality to the medical science community. COVID-19 has verified the continued structural problems that have plagued America's policies, beliefs, and practices — specifically its power dynamics, hierarchical stratification, and structural racism. Sociologist Lynn Weber, writing in her book, *Understanding Race, Class, Gender, and Sexuality*, describes the dominance in a system as, "The power to define the rules, be advantaged by the rules, and the ability to name the game, i.e., interpret the outcome."

In the American game of power, there are approximately 100,000,000 minorities at the bottom rung of the income, justice, and equality ladder. To complicate matters further, minorities are concentrated in food desert areas with limited access to healthy food due to household income, distance from a supermarket, lack of transportation, or the availability of healthy food in local stores, making them susceptible to underlying health conditions. Four of the top ten leading causes of death today — coronary heart disease, diabetes, stroke, and cancer — are chronic diseases with well-established links to diet.

While reeling from the realization that the structural inequality produced the underlying health conditions that resulted in 70% of COVID-19 deaths being minorities, old-fashioned structural racism reared its ugly head in the murder of George Floyd. Floyd's death provides the inescapable context to the larger frameworks of prejudice and inequality within American society and the impetus for change. COVID-19 and Floyd's death bring several inequalities, beliefs, and practices into our field of vision at the same time.

Addressing structural racism at all levels must take place through education and awareness of racist terms and practices, avoiding and combating stereotypes, and celebrating differences. Structural racism necessarily requires addressing the various levels of inequality that result in the absence of structural equality. Structural equality is rooted in a vision of a just society based in an ethic of courtesy, humility, tolerance for others, and love that moves and motivates individuals and communities to affirm everyone's self-worth in the face of pervasive dehumanization.

As a descendant of old-fashioned racism and the entanglement of New Jim Crow laws in the criminal justice system with marginal relief in sight, my story is a bit different. I am confined in society's house of inequalities. I am vulnerable to suffer the collateral damage of the MDC and society's prejudices during this COVID-19 pandemic because I am a stroke survivor.

TICKET TO RIDE

BOUDICCA

Here at Camp Prisoney Land, I have the privilege of
working in the law library. My office is a haven of
serenity. I love the job. Really. Love. It. There are
many benefits: freedom of movement on the compound, an
air-conditioned office during our Everglades summers, a
desk job with a comfy chair, unlimited access to books
in the general library, and I like to help people.

As a citizen, you only get so much free representation
in court by an attorney. If you are in prison you get
assigned someone like me, a law clerk, trained at the
expense of the Department of Corrections. I am not an
attorney, my purpose is to get you another look from the
court and an evidentiary hearing where you can get a
licensed attorney.

Another benefit of the job is I get to tell people what
to do. There is a huge ego stroke when someone who
didn't take my advice says to me, "Boudicca, if only I
had done what you told me to do, I would not now be in
this terrible position." Oh yeah that gives me a zing!

When a client offers compensation, I do not accept. No
thanks, you are generous but I must decline. There are
many law clerk buses in Camp Prisoney Land, but there
is only one Boudicca bus. I'm the driver. If someone pays
me, they think they are qualified to drive the bus. I
tell you when to get on, where to sit, and — most impor-
tantly — when to get off. No one is driving this bus into
a ditch. Everyone on my bus will get to their destina-
tion on time.

You could say I'm independent. I like to help but don't like being helped. And then I got COVID-19. Hauled ignobly to the infirmary, thrown into an isolation cell with a mattress on a filthy floor. The infection worsened. I was getting three shots in the fundament every day and gasping through an oxygen mask.

Finally, I started recovering but I was weak as a kitten. I was decanted back to Plague Dorm D. First I had to traverse the compound one painful step at a time. Everything in my body hurt. I could not carry the weight of my property stuffed in a cheap plastic garbage bag. I dragged it behind me, feeling like I was climbing Mount Everest without enough oxygen. Gasp, gasp, trudge, trudge, drag, drag.

My energy drained out. I stopped right in front of Plague Dorm D and sat on the bag. The door was only a few feet away. It might as well have been miles. I heard the scrape of an officer's key twisting the lock. Great, I thought to myself, all I need is for some Morelock officer to come out screaming at me.

Instead, the door burst open, and there were my fellow inmates crowded in the doorway, shouting encouragement. "Come on Boudicca! You can make it just a few more steps!" Summoning the last of my strength I dragged everything over and collapsed in their arms. The women grabbed all my stuff, and me, then carried me up to my new cell. It had been thoroughly cleaned and reeked of bleach and mango-fresh air deodorizer.

It's all a blur but someone dragged in a good mattress and a puffy pillow. Another made my bed. A third woman sorted my possessions and put them away in my locker. A hot sweet cup of tea was placed in my hand.

I was too weak to resist. I couldn't even say, "No, thanks, you are too generous but I must decline." Instead of driving the bus, I was riding.

INSTEAD
OF
DRIVING
THE
BUS
I
WAS
RIDING

A FLORIDA INMATE'S COVID HAIKU

MARTIN VANN

Two to a table
Social distance please, masks on
Coronavirus

Florida must open now!
Setting new records again
Trump loves Desantis

No tests done here
Hundreds likely positive
They don't want to know

Law library closed
Legal deadlines come and gone
Sorry, case dismissed

Eight months since it hit
We've got something here you don't
Herd immunity

THROW AWAY
THE KEYS PLEASE

DAVE BECKER

At the time of this writing, I've been locked up for
8,851 days or 24 years, two months, three weeks, three
days. I know men who have spent many more years in this
hollow place, but time is relative and my time spent
incarcerated is, in my estimation, sufficient for me
to have learned my lesson. Considering all of this,
however, I can say with a degree of certainty that
there is hardly a place I would rather be while the
world outside these gates falls apart. Prison, for all
intents and purposes, has finally become an agreeable
location to wait out the storm.

I watch it all unfold on my prison television screen.
The virus is a ruthless killer of both weak and strong.
COVID-19 destroys life, economies, social order, common
sense, and even the typically unassailable arena of
professional sports. The world outside, where everything I want is purposely kept from my grasp, is
beginning to look more like the world where I live. I
never would've thought that my whole family would be on
a mandated lockdown or that they would have to follow
strict guidelines while maneuvering through grocery
stores. These are the things that I usually get to
share with my family — how it is to be incarcerated —
but now they seem to have better stories than I do.

My aunt told me how she almost came to blows with
another lady in the grocery store because the other
lady wasn't wearing a mask and she was creeping up on
my aunt (who has lung issues). I haven't had a good
fight story to tell in months and my family is out there
in the free world ready to scrap over things that

normally would not bother them. This virus has pilfered my thunder and turned my family into hardcore thugs.

But I still wonder if being in here isn't better. I mean, in prison, my rent always gets paid and my utilities are never shut off. The food, although sometimes questionable, never fails to materialize from that slot in the chow hall wall. That's not even to mention the 24-hour security force, here for my protection and to ensure that everybody is in compliance with the face mask policy.

If COVID-19 isn't enough to make one appreciate prison, society has decided to detonate the social justice bomb after the unfortunate murder of George Floyd. For a moment, the COVID-19 issue takes a sideline seat as images of riots and protests are painted across the television screen.

I can't tell whom I'm expected to hate in this conflict; however, I understand that I am expected to hate someone.

In prison, the reactions to these issues are merely manifested as sideway glances or unsavory grunts. Nobody is burning down the only eating establishment or looting the local grocery outlet. Nobody is fighting over who has the right to tell someone (anyone?) else what to do. Reactions to social issues mostly belong to those who are not incarcerated. I guess we simply feel that we have no control and so why suffer the unsavory taste of complaint?

And I'm good with all of that because to tell you the truth, I just want my three meals and my warm bunk and my limited access to the canteen where I can spend money I don't have on crap I don't need. I'm not so melancholy at the idea of being incarcerated while the world out there smolders.

Maybe I'm institutionalized to the point where I have zero appetite for conflict. If that's the case, then somebody deserves a promotion because they've incarcerated the fight out of me. Or maybe I've just been dwelling down here at rock bottom so long that the recurring grievances of society sound like inordinate drivel in my ear because I have truly learned what is valuable in life.

Out in the free world, it seems the virus is only taken seriously as long as the masses feel that they're getting their fair share of mindless entertainment and raging consumerism. As soon as the virus becomes inconvenient and bothersome, the intensity of its deadliness becomes questionable and suspect. It seems as if the real issue everybody is avoiding is the mental acuity of the planet's least restricted society.

Either way, I finally feel that I'm at an advantage being in prison, as if maybe the uninhibited population is missing out on the good life. This is quite a contrast to how I felt in the pre-COVID-19 days.

I believe that my sentence was deserved and I appreciate the opportunity to get a second chance. But my release date is fast approaching and I'm honestly beginning to wonder if getting out is what is best for me. Sure, after doing multiple years in prison, the ideas of release and freedom are overwhelmingly enticing, but "overwhelmingly enticing" doesn't quite amount to "tremendously sensible." What am I supposed to do if the virus finds me out there? Here, there is an army of tough nurses ready to attend to my medical needs.

All in all, I feel safe in this place. Until the population can figure out how to make society a place worth living in again, well, then maybe you could do me a favor and just keep me locked up and throw away the keys, please.

BLIND SESTINAS ARE INVISIBLE IN THE DICTIONARY

TIBNI RETH

In the midst of a worldwide pandemic,
life and work were expected to be perfect.
Out of nowhere, an enemy came
unseen to create a "passing" problem like magic.
From which in the ultimate,
a person should have much gratitude.
Then, all mandated isolation and hunker-down
orders evolved into forced domesticity.
While all the stores which feed domestic dreams
go bankrupt like wild.
Unthinkable that everyone turned
into a housewife, even the species of male.

Gone are home stores like Bed Bath and Beyond;
also Pier One, all gone like magic.
Revealing in secret that the one crying the
hardest & loudest is the manly male!
Perhaps, then, he won't be required to be
a king of domesticity.
He is to accept what he is turning into with gratitude.
When all he wants to do is to attend
happy hour and go hog wild.
As everyone knows what a boy considers
days or nights that are perfect.

When the homebound guy is...
well, home, he won't think it's wild.
To look up what sestina means, even when it sounds like
another 's' word that's perfect.
With one too proud to ask for directions —
quite like the typical male.
Whatever is not found,
he still finds it best to have gratitude.

What's so twisted is his idea of domesticity
Became a search for sestina that's invisible in
the dictionary, fantastically thinking like magic.

Okay, Okay. This is not a day of bashing the male.
Neither is it a day to criticize the virtues
or vices of domesticity.
And it is ever a day for perfectionists to
strive to be perfect.
Like the saying that declares you can't be too
rich or too thin — you can't have too much gratitude.
Believe that the thought is not too wild.
In a world that does not believe in magic.

A typical guy is too logical to believe in magic.
The quintessential "tough dude"
is averse to domesticity.
They must love order that's wild.
What he deems perfect
Most females cannot regard with gratitude.
So for any other,
it's most difficult to define what's male.

For all my bitching and complaining,
I miss my brilliant friends who are male.
When I cannot resort to magic
I am left with a strong dose of gratitude.
The perfect panacea for what in the
world is not perfect.
One day, I plan to go wild.
In the most tranquil & harmonious domesticity.
What I wrote is my idea of a perfect home —
so full of magic.

Of a loosely-defined and chaotically-ordered
wild domesticity.
Shared with a bright male type who has
in the heart much gratitude.

THE BROKEN HOME SYNDROME

GERVASIO TORRES

Never did I imagine a family could be formed in this environment, but one did. A ragtag bunch of "societal misfits" joined together and we evolved. And then dissolved.

Whether someone arrived only a few months ago or had been a longtime resident, those living on side two of the Alpha Top dorm at Everglades Correctional had become a family. A personal tragedy brought prayers and words of sympathy. Holiday meals were made with everyone in mind, regardless of someone's financial status. Education was strongly encouraged, as several current, and former, educational facilitators were on hand to tutor. We had our own craftsman of cards for any occasion: degree-seeking psychologists, avid sports gurus, encouragers, uncles.

In the wake of the pandemic, both sides of Alpha Top were converted into a dormitory for orderlies who would be at a higher risk of bringing the virus into the institution since they were having regular contact with employees and other civilian personnel. If infected, staff could quarantine the resident(s) and contain the potential spread to other parts of the compound.

So, on April 2, 2020, the transfers, or as some residents referred to them, "evictions," began. Over the course of a couple weeks, an officer would arrive at our wing with what was dubbed "Schindler's List." Only a few names a day were called. Each time we grew anxious and wondered if our name would be called and, if so, where we would go. One resident said, "It was like waiting to enter the gas chamber."

Life in prison is continually filled with uncertainties, yet the one thing we seek comfort in is where we lay our heads at night. We develop a circle of trust for the people in our immediate surroundings. Being removed from that safety net wreaks havoc on the mind, body, and soul. What may seem inconsequential to some means the world to those of us who experience it firsthand.

Our 'community' was disbanded for what was felt to be a higher purpose. I cannot deny it was done for the greater good, but what about those left to fend for themselves without that sense of family unity? What or who will keep them on track?

Most everyone has gone their separate ways. For a select few, the move proved to be a good thing. Others mourned the loss of people who would be there when others weren't.

We're still in prison, but for a time we were able to coexist. We knew each other's names. We felt as though someone truly cared. We were able to gain back some of the things we'd lost from what seems like a lifetime ago.

I CAN'T STAND TALKING ABOUT THE CORONAVIRUS, AND OTHER COMPLAINTS

RYAN M. MOSER

I wish that I could go back in time and erase the word "coronavirus" from the vocabulary of human beings, that I could become an astrophysicist, solely with the intent of opening a wormhole in the fabric of space and time in order to dump the title "COVID-19" into the infinite ether of another dimension. I'd make it illegal to say the word "quarantine." If I had the ability, I would censor the news media pandemic coverage to just the facts. I would definitely require that anyone calling themselves an "expert" on infectious disease or recession or personal protective equipment or supply chains or contact tracing or digital messaging or hospital administration be vetted for some degree of serious credentials in said topic or field. I would like to eradicate the term *social distancing* from the face of the earth. I'd sleep better at night if I could beat the shit out of my clingy face mask.

I hate hearing about the coronavirus. I can't stand talking about it. As a writer, I rolled my eyes when asked to write about the pandemic. As a son and father and brother, I listened compassionately to my family as they described their new way of life filled with worry, but as soon as I hung up the phone...I cursed. That's all they want to talk about some days. I'm not a sociopath or a misanthrope who doesn't care about the world; I love people and practice random acts of kindness every day — it's the goddamn coronavirus that I despise. I have to watch the news every day because, as a prisoner, that is my lifeline to the outside, but I physically contort in my seat when I

listen to every reporter drone on about this unexpected killer for the 106th day in a row. I get it,
this is serious and many have died. I'm empathetic to
their suffering. But if I could just throw a shoe at the
television screen, I would feel a little bit better.

Fear mongering makes my cortisol shoot through the
roof. Unintelligent people should be prevented from
causing mass hysteria. If you tell me this is the end
of the world, I will most likely want to punch you in
the nose, or at the very least turn away dramati-
cally with a civilized harrumph. Evolutionary biology
has proven that we as a species are very hard to anni-
hilate — I'm personally more worried about oil wars or
bigotry or an environmental crisis caused by greed and
more rain than a pathogen. This isn't *I Am Legend* or
World War Z. Here's a newsflash for you, courtesy of Bob
Marley: *Everything's Gonna Be Alright*. I promise. You
don't have to scare people more than they already are.

If COVID-19 were a person, it would be the worst boss
I've ever had. The psycho ex-girlfriend who cut all
the sleeves off my dress shirts. My 11th grade teacher
who encouraged me to quit school. That person would
be Hitler incarnate or the prick who stole my parking
spot in the city every day for a year. I would frame
them for a murder. Give out their Social Security number
on 4chan and sign them up for a multi-level marketing
campaign. I would make it my personal life mission
to destroy every atom in their existence through any
means necessary, and laugh about it afterwards.

Harsh? Maybe. Justified? Definitely.

I'm not flippant about the death and devastation
caused by my nemesis. It's just that I refuse to
live my life in fear. I'm aware of how serious the
pandemic is; it has taken over the world, but I don't
have to let it take over my thoughts and speech.

I won't let it live in my mind and burrow into my brain like a bad idea. I will keep it at a distance, like a weird roommate or a coworker with halitosis. I will take precautions, respect other people's personal space, wash my hands, honor the dead, hope for the living, encourage positivity, and wait.

That is all I can do.

What I won't do is talk about you anymore, coronavirus.

Asshole.

LESMES CASERES ————————————————————————————————

THE CONVICT WONDERS WHICH STAFF MEMBER COULD KILL HIM

→

IN MEMORIAM: 2020'S COVID-19 LOSSES TO THE DEATH ROW COMMUNITY

BOB R. (COWBOY) WILLIAMS JR.

It's rather sad, and pretty enlightening, being on Death
Row. I mean every day you wake up and you know exactly
what your reality is. Regardless if it will happen or
not, the cold hard fact, at least for me, is that they
are going to kill me one day. They are going to take me
to a funky room, strap me to a bed, stick needles into my
arms, then after opening a "viewing curtain" so people
can watch, they are going to pump five to seven grams of
liquid fire into my body until I am graveyard dead.

That cold hard reality, however, gives me something
special. Facing it, wrestling with it, coming to terms
with it, even accepting it, up to a point that is, makes
each and every moment, each interaction with another
person...everything...into something so, so, special, and
of value of the greatest worth.

And then, something comes along, something we can't
really even square up to and fight. I mean the death
penalty I can fight through the courts. But this new
thing from distant shores just showed up like a thief
in the night. Man, you can't even see it.

Now, most folks see home as a place. I don't. Home,
to me, is people. It's where you see those around you
reflected in yourself, and yourself reflected in those
around you. I've been here at San Quentin since late
1996. Got here when I was just 20 years old. This place
will never be my HOME, but it has become sort of home
nonetheless. COVID-19 came into my home and left with a
few of my friends and associates; heck, since this is a

sort of home, it took part of the family. Sadly, it took the following men:

RICHARD STITELY. An old fella with a bit of Texas in his talk. Called him Godfather sometimes, or Trog (meaning Troglodyte). Played cards with him almost every day for a good 15 years while he was on my yard. The guy's ears would kinda flap when he shook his head. Guess they done flapped him on home.

JOHNNY AVILA. From down around Fresno. Spent years on the yard with him. Quick tempered, kind of short, but not a bad dude. Used to read a Native American legend or two at A.M.I. services.

MANUEL ALVAREZ. Big 'ole kat from Cuba. Called him Cuba, too, or Elián (after Elián González from the early 2000s). Ole boy, spoke okay English, but when he got all riled up, man, he couldn't speak a lick of English no more because all the Cubano came out. Used to like the Yankees. Only he could never pronounce "Yankees" right. The man would say Jankees! Ole Elián is swimmin' home.

DWAYNE CARY. A good brother from down around L.A. way. Played basketball with him and against him. He had a little game, too. Started E.B.A.C. along with him as well. The man was a United States Navy Veteran. Well, fair winds and following waters, I'll stand and salute the flag for you.

JOSEPH CORDOVA. Didn't know him personally, but I would see him at the same table and in the same seat on the yard playing cards. He rolled around in a wheelchair, and I believe they called him Geezer. Roll on, old son.

TROY ASHMUS. Called him Humphrey for reasons unknown to me, though I wish I had thought to ask. Creative as all get out, too. Give him some beads and maybe a bit of leather, and the dude would come up with all sorts of cool stuff.

JEFFREY HAWKINS. Old school convict. Seemed like he had been doing time since he was just a kid. Good man though, and he had a good heart. He's free now.

JOHN BEAMES. We called him JB. Big fella with a mane of hair you could see from way way afar and he always had a smile. The guy bought me some art supplies one time for no other reason than he heard I needed some, and I barely knew him then, too! Things like that help one remember that we are still human after all.

DAVID REED, SCOTT ERSKINE, LONNIE FRANKLIN, JOHN ABEL, AND THOMAS POTTS. I can't for sure say if I knew them all or not; then again, they, like so many of us, might have had a nickname and that's what I would have known them by. Nonetheless, they all, I am certain, contributed to the ambiance that can only be found here on Death Row in whatever way they could...

All these men, and maybe more, were taken from us prematurely by a microscopic virus they couldn't even see to go to battle against. In their own ways they will be remembered and missed. See you fellers on the other side of them Pearly Gates, just don't be trying to chip up the streets of gold and go sticking the chips in your socks. Heck, wait 'til I get there at least.

See, these men all came here for whatever it was they came here for. And, after many years, and a whole lot of thought, I've come to realize that whatever it was that a man may have done, didn't do, and left undone in his past life before coming to prison and/or Death Row, no longer matters in the same way. Maybe they took a life, or two...but after years spent here where they took none, they stopped being murderers. They were no longer to be judged by those honest - maybe - and rather harsh, standards that dang near all convicts and ex-cons are so often judged by.

Think about this. I mean, if you once got caught cheating on a test at school, would you like to be known as a cheater, along with seemingly forever being judged as such, for the rest of your life, even if you never once did it again? Most people recoil at that and pretty vociferously think, "Heck no!"

Well, these guys came here and, it is my most fervent belief, changed. They grew up and matured, they evolved, and they found some sort of redemption, and rehabilitation that made them into better Men, Human Beings, Children of God, and just plain old decent Fellas.

So, it became, or becomes, not about whatever you did, didn't do, and left undone, but about what you do with it. How you honor it in a good and higher way. How you learn from it all and share that learning. How you strive to make it all mean something a little less on the human level, and much more on the level of the Divine. I, for one, just have to believe that these men, friends of a sort, even family members in some convoluted way, touched the lives of the men in here and lives out of here, too, especially mine, in their own ways, and that they found their own meaning, their own purpose, right here in this dank and dark Earthbound Purgatory. God bless them all for it. May these men all rest in peace, fly with angels, and pop up in our minds now and then.

TRAVIS R. MONN

"

HE LIVED IN A CELL WHERE HIS NAME WAS A NUMBER AND HIS ONLY PLEASURES WERE THE THINGS HE'D REMEMBER

"

COVID-19 VS THE MOUNTAIN

EDWARD DeMORETA

COVID-19 has done nothing to my day. Nor can it. If one man in prison is infected or one thousand, it makes no difference. Breakfast at 5:30am. Lunch at 11am. Dinner at 3:30pm. My days are the mountain standing against the elements. Unmoved. Perhaps superficially changed in some tiny way but unquestionably the mountain remains.

BULLSEYE

ERIC FINLEY

JUNE 29
So far one man has tested positive in this dorm. He was removed this morning and an official has just come to notify us we are on lockdown quarantine.

Until today, this dorm housed the kitchen workers for this facility; this is probably not a good thing.

Another testing site was set up today, and it looked like the other side of the compound was being tested.

As we watched, two inmates in line began fighting. At this distance, details are hard to discern, but it looked like one man was stabbing the other. They were both handcuffed and removed.

It's now after 9 PM, we've not been given dinner yet.

A short while ago, the first inmate who tested positive returned to retrieve his property and visit briefly.

JUNE 30
Lunch was at 2 PM. There was a delay due to cleaning up vomit. As the food arrived, a man began to throw up. He was removed, we ate, then he returned.

JULY 1
Officers and medical staff now wear foot coverings, bodysuits, gloves, and double masks, some with face shields. All carry electronic panic buttons, sergeants also carry pepper spray.

Another man was removed for observation.

JULY 2

Three separate buildings on quarantine had recreation together on the yard today.

The last man removed for observation was back. He's been back for about six hours. He has no mattress, sheets, blanket or anything else. As I write this, he is sweating and sleeping on the plain steel bed frame. He was born in 1941, and is 78 years of age.

10:15 PM. I just watched three inmates put an unresponsive man with fixed eyes on a gurney and take him away at a rather leisurely pace. Two frightened looking medical staff arrived; neither touched him.

Now the 78-year-old has a mattress.

JULY 3

Breakfast at noon. Lunch at 7 PM. Dinner at 11:30 PM, it's spoiled.

JULY 4

It's midnight, no dinner yet. Lots of coughing and sneezing going on. Dinner arrived a bit after 1 AM, actually on the 5th.

JULY 5

Doors were opened today for five minutes "to create airflow." Lunch at 8:30 PM. Dinner around 2 AM. Some meals are rancid upon arrival, none are hot.

It is a volatile environment here, like we are stuck in a Robin Cook or Stephen King novel.

Our talk is no longer of the world, it's about conditions here, and survival.

THE HEARTS, MINDS AND STOMACHS OF GROWN-ASS MEN

JOE GARCIA

I'm stuck in an isolation cell, quarantined away from the mainline prison population. Still, I can clearly see San Quentin corrections officers struggling within their new COVID-19 workplace reality — right along with the community under their control.

"Staffing shortages have resulted in restricted movement for the entire population and a disruption in the services you all deserve and expect," Acting Warden Ron Broomfield wrote in a memorandum distributed to prisoners on the evening of July 9, 2020.

From the third tier of an ADSEG (Administrative Segregation) housing unit, all I need to do is listen. Officers walk past my cell, discussing with one another how the program is supposed to run. Lately, these aren't the regular officers assigned to the unit.

I can't say whether it's true or not, but one morning I heard prisoners downstairs talking about how their tier officer got called to the front desk and sent home — a fresh victim of a positive test result.

ADSEG has its own way of doing things. To be escorted to the shower stall, we must first place our hands behind our backs at the open tray slot of our cell. Officers reach in and cuff us before they unlock the cell door. That's the protocol.

In my three-plus years living in San Quentin's North Block prior to being rehoused, I never once saw any officers armed with rifles and walking along inside the building's observation scaffolding, ready for action. Here in ADSEG, a gunner is always on shift on the third-floor level, pacing back and forth.

On shower days, I see my neighbors being escorted one-by-one past my cell in their boxers and sandals, hands shackled behind their backs. The officers uncuff us only after they lock us inside the shower. It's also the only time we can be issued a state razor, which we must return within minutes. The gunner stays vigilant, standing guard during every person's escort to and from the shower.

But most of us being housed here right now are NOT here for any disciplinary reasons. We're here because of the COVID-19 outbreak and the lack of adequate spacing. Me, I've never had a single RVR (Rules Violation Report) during my entire incarceration. This is my first stay in any prison's Hole.

There are guys here all around me who came from Chino's California Institute for Men (CIM) and brought the coronavirus with them. There are guys here who came directly from county jails following their convictions. And there are guys here like me — removed from the mainline and placed in isolated quarantine.

We're all stuck here indefinitely. As frustrating as it is for us, I think it actually might be the safest spot to be right now.

Just feeding our population of almost 4,000 incarcerated residents has proved difficult for the San Quentin staff. For three and a half days straight, we were given nothing but box lunches for breakfast, lunch and dinner.

Packaged at another prison somewhere and shipped here, these meals consisted primarily of either bologna or cheese, with some bread, crackers and cookies —

100% processed food, sealed in individual plastic. Even the ubiquitous staple of peanut butter and jelly has disappeared.

It's not the tier officers' fault. All they can do is distribute whatever the kitchen sends their way, but these officers bear the brunt of all the complaints and yelling.

"I'm sick, fighting this virus," I heard a prisoner yell out from his cell. "How the fuck am I supposed to get better eating this shit?"

On the morning of July 10, 2020, I awoke to a loudspeaker announcement at 6:45 a.m.: "Listen up. Your breakfast today, it looks like there's a yogurt, a boiled egg already peeled, some fruit and a pack of hot sauce. Take everything out of the container it comes in and give the container back. We need those back."

The announcement seemed to break the levee of angst and bitterness amongst some of my neighbors.

"Fuck you! Feed that shit to your kids," one guy screamed from somewhere below me. "We're grown-ass men up in here and y'all feeding us what — a goddamn Happy Meal?"

"Do your motherfuckin' job and bring me a 602 with that shit!"

A 602 [six-oh-two] is the standardized California Department of Corrections and Rehabilitation (CDCR) form prisoners must fill out to file an official grievance.

"I'm serious right now, y'all," the same prisoner continued, addressing everyone within earshot. "All of us need to stop lying down and accepting this shit. We all need to start filing 602s every goddamn day. Make them fix this shit."

I could hear the officer who made the breakfast announcement confront the man face-to-face at his cell door.

"I can't control what they give us to feed you guys. You know that," the officer said for all to hear. "I'm just giving you a heads up, and you say, 'Fuck me'?"

"Hey man, if you were living in this cell, getting these meals, you'd be pissed right now, too," the prisoner continued. "Y'all come to work here every day and see what's going on, but you ain't feelin' us right now."

"We do feel you, believe me," the officer fired back. "We're dealing with all this shit, too. They just spent $7.5 million on an outside vendor to provide meals for the next 30 days. I'm just trying to keep you guys updated. You want a 602? I'll bring all you guys a 602 whenever you want one."

The endless barrage of adamant voices can be maddening. If my headphones aren't bumping my music full blast, I'll be forced to listen to these constant tirades all day. Thank God for Taylor Swift.

Most of the guys doing all the talking are short-timers — guys who've been incarcerated for a year or two here, a few years there. Lately, their incessant yapping turns frequently to Governor Gavin Newsom and CDCR Secretary Ralph Diaz's recent promises to release as many prisoners as early as possible to alleviate the overcrowding. In the short time I've been over here in ADSEG, about a dozen prisoners have been called for early release — a few each morning, sometimes. Too bad it's these low-grade offenders who inevitably drive the recidivism rates up and reflect poorly on those of us hoping for a chance at parole.

Usually, one way or another, we'd get breakfast and lunch all at once in the morning. But starting July 10, they delivered our lunch separately, around 11 a.m. — what looked like a chain restaurant's pasta entrée, like something from Olive Garden.

"I don't hear y'all yelling about 602s no more," a prisoner commented along the tier. "I ain't gonna lie. This shit's kinda good."

The response to the new meal plan grew more positive at dinner time with an entrée of creamy grilled chicken and vegetables.

"I don't even feel like I'm locked up right now," one guy said loudly as he enjoyed his food.

Last week, one officer worked my tier alone. He delivered the paltry meals apologetically, came back around to pick up our trash, handed out toilet paper and soap, and made sure everyone got a shower. Two officers usually share these duties.

"You knocked it all out by yourself," I told him as he escorted me back after my shower. "I'm impressed."

"We're all in this together," he said with sincerity in his voice. "The virus affects all of us — in here and out there. I'm barely holding it together."

The officer said it was his third double in a row. "They keep mandating all these extra shifts on us right now."

I asked him if he fears catching the coronavirus from the San Quentin community.

"It is what it is. I've got to be right back here at 6 a.m., so I'll be lucky if I get three hours of solid sleep. That'll wreak havoc on your immune system's strength, for sure. But I'm here now."

It's been over a week, and I haven't seen that officer since. I hope he's doing alright, wherever he is.

SICK

JOLLY ROGER

Last night I was told that my friend had to be resus-
citated twice; they don't think she will survive the
night. It's June 1, 2020. We have been on lockdown
since March. Well, some sort of lockdown. At first they
only stopped us from going to recreation together and
eating together. They would take one dorm at a time
to the "chow" hall, ignoring the fact that we were
not infected and that the greatest threat comes from
the staff members. I worked in maintenance and was
surprised they were allowing inmates to continue to
work closely with staff members.

On Wednesday, April 15, 2020, almost a month into this,
they began a series of mass movements on the whole
compound to segregate everyone based upon their work
assignment. Throughout this campaign, which was blamed
on Tallahassee — they blame everything on Tallahassee
— about half the compound was moved around from dorm
to dorm for about two weeks. People who had been living
in their assigned areas were uprooted; they were moving
people daily, well into the night sometimes. Madness.

During this time the first case was reported.

Rumor has it a certain officer entered the prison
knowing he was symptomatic. Officers are ordered to
do rounds every 15 minutes and search 12 people per
shift. They touch every door, open every curtain, pat
search, and delve into lockers. This practice was not
curtailed. Women out of Echo dorm complained of symptoms and were taken to medical and tested. All of them
tested positive. The administration ordered tests for
the whole dorm and out of 100 people, 79 inmates tested

positive. More than half the dorm had been moved out and spread around the compound, effectively spreading the virus as well. As a result, they had to lock down three more dorms. Tests were ordered for the whole compound. More than 235 inmates tested positive and today my friend is on a ventilator.

We have been on some sort of lockdown since the 21st of March, with no end in sight.

We are allowed one hour per week outside. We are fed one hot meal and two cold meals a day — baloney, peanut butter, bread and more bread — at erratic times. They threaten us with quarantine extensions if we ask for Tylenol. They say inmates are masking symptoms, yet we have not been retested.

What will happen to my friend if the administration is the only voice she has? Be strong.

...

Editor's Note: Jolly Roger's friend passed away from COVID-19 shortly after this was written. The author of this piece prefers to use a pseudonym because of repercussions from past pieces published under her real name. For that reason we omitted the name of her friend who died.

FLORIDA SET TO REDUCE STATE PRISON POPULATION BY COVID-19 DEATHS

GLENN SMITH

Coronavirus. COVID-19. I didn't know how this virus was named until I got the May 2020 issue of *Prison Legal News* a few days ago — amazing in itself since this is only the second issue allowed in by the Florida Department of Corrections (FDC) in the past three years or so. It is now June, 2020, at Dade Correctional Institution (DCI), Florida City, Florida.

It doesn't appear that the virus is loose here yet, but it seems more inevitable each day, since cases in Florida are now rising. This state may become the epicenter of viral infection in the US, according to the news media.

And Miami-Dade County has the highest infection/death rate in Florida. Scary.

I think each man is asking himself, "Will I survive?"

My opinion is that when the virus hits here, we'll definitely know because we'll have 400 deaths in quick succession. This is an American with Disabilities Act (ADA) compound, so there is a higher proportion of inmates with medical problems here than at other institutions: respiratory, cardiovascular disease, compromised immune systems, liver disease, diabetes, obesity, dementia, and old age.

And we are packed in. I'm in one of the five open bay dorms with two wings each. The wing I'm in was designed to accommodate 48 inmates. By Florida statute the legal capacity is 72 inmates — 150% of the design capacity — and that's how many inmates are usually housed here.

Bunks — metal frames with a sheet-metal construct for the mattress, a thin, futon-like pad — are in a barrack-line atmosphere with an approximately 40'x70' sleeping area. Double bunks (built about 40 inches between upper and lower bunks) are arranged along walls approximately 36 inches apart with 12 inches between the center area of two rows of single bunks (the wheelchair bound, 16 inmates). Social distancing under these conditions could only be a joke; we've been ordered to sleep head to toe.

If the virus were here, the arrangement would be futile in reducing its spread because the air circulated between the few windows that open, the exhaust fan, and the ceiling fans, would be virus-ridden.

The sanitation area is about 25×30 feet with seven toilets, six urinals, 12 sinks, and eight showers, including one with handicap seating.

Our "day room" is approximately 15×30 feet with one T.V. and bench seating for 24 if maxed out: two tables seating seven, one kiosk for tablet use with a chair. There are also two drinking fountains with cold water, one hot. Orders have been issued to clean and wipe down common areas every hour. Only the restroom/shower area is cleaned about five times a day. No extra soap is provided at sinks for hand washing. A single small bar of soap (1¼"x2"x1¼") is issued per week to each inmate. This is not adequate for even the daily showers required, let alone more hand-washing for COVID-19 prophylaxis.

Inmates have all been issued two cloth Florida Department of Corrections (FDC) constructed face masks with instructions to wear one all the time except when showering, sleeping, brushing teeth, or eating. While FDC officials may think this futile effort is fooling anyone into thinking an effort is being made to protect inmates from viral infection, it is rather evidence of officials' stupid thinking and lack of integrity in any real effort to protect us.

The virus is only going to come into the institution through FDC staff. Outside volunteer programs have been suspended. Visitation has been suspended. Practically all programs have been suspended: religious, educational, and general library. No one is coming into contact with inmates except medical, kitchen, maintenance, and correctional staff, all of whom are supposed to be wearing masks all the time. But they don't. Nor do they practice social distancing.

So what's the point of the instructions to inmates?

Inmate kitchen workers are generally not wearing masks. Food trades are handled by many when serving. There is no dishwashing machine. Few inmates (i.e. slave labor) handwashing cups, sporks, and trays actually care about sanitizing requirements. The medical/multi service waiting area is too small to provide any practical social distancing. There is never any soap in the inmate restroom for hand washing. There are also six-foot marks on sidewalks for lining up. That social distancing lasted about two days.

But again, what's the point?

Inmates in "secure housing units" are doubled up two to a cell designed for one man (again, as legal capacity per Florida statute), about 72 square feet. These dorms have three wings of 32 cells per wing. Forced air ventilation provides most air circulation. These systems have never been cleaned. There are three secure housing units on this compound. And every inmate on the south side of the compound in open bay dorms must utilize one barbershop to conform to FDC grooming rules.

As almost all Florida State prisons operate at legal capacity, the only solution is to release prisoners. The only really legally applicable release mechanism in Florida that might address release of a practical number of prisoners is commutation of each sentence. That only happens by a majority vote of the Florida Board of Executive Clemency (Governor, Attorney General, Chief Financial Officer, Secretary of Agriculture — the Cabinet).

This probably will not happen as the number involved would overwhelm the mechanism. The Board would have to sit for months to review cases of more than 93,000 inmates.

And we are generally kept in the dark concerning the status of COVID-19 in the prison system. Although Mark Inch, the Florida Secretary of Corrections, initially emailed inmates with tablets or kiosk access and told us that the FDC website would post such information, inmates cannot directly access the Internet to verify that this is so. No email updates have been made. The media rarely reports the status of COVID-19 in Florida prisons. But Governor DeSantis's press conferences have attributed infection spikes in some counties to its prisons.

It now seems likely that neither visitation nor program operation will be reinstated until COVID-19 vaccinations are available to the public, FDC staff, and inmates. Although inmates are a vulnerable population, it is unlikely that inmate vaccinations would be prioritized, though they would be among the first in a medical paradigm. The FDC doesn't even give flu vaccinations in a timely manner, if ever. I specifically requested one in September 2019 and did not receive one until March 2020, and then only by an extraordinary effort on my part.

Nothing being done here will halt COVID-19's wild-fire-like spread and a practically instantaneous wave of deaths of the most vulnerable inmates, myself included. I am 71 years old.

Florida Set to Reduce State Prison
Population by COVID-19 Deaths

COrona VIrus Disease - 2019. COVID-19. I didn't
know how this virus was named until I got the May 2020
issue of Prison Legal News a few days ago — amazing
in itself since this is only the second issue allowed in by
the Florida Department of Corrections (FDC) in the past 3
years or so. It is now June 2020 at Dade Correctional
Institution (Dade CI), Florida City, Florida.

It doesn't appear that the virus is loose here yet, but it
seems more inevitable each day that it will be, since cases in
Florida are now increasing at a rate that Florida may now
become the epicenter of viral infection in the U.S according
to news media. And Miami-Dade County has the highest
infection/death rate in Florida. Scary.

I think each man is asking himself, "Will I
survive?" My opinion is that when the virus hits here
we'll definitely know because we'll have 400 deaths in
quick succession of those here with comorbidity conditions —
respiratory problems, cardiovascular disease, compromised
immune systems, liver disease, diabetes, obesity, dementia,
old age. This is an ADA (American with Disabilities
Act) compound. So there is a higher proportion of inmates
with medical problems here than at other institutions.

And we are packed in. I'm in an "open bay"
"dorm" housing unit. The wing I'm in was designed to
accomodate 48 inmates. By Florida Statute the legal
capacity is 72 inmates (150% of design capacity) and
that's how many inmates are actually usually housed.
Inmates are stacked on top of each other in double
bunks in a barracklike atmosphere in an approximately
40' x 70' sleeping area. Double bunks (built about
40" between upper and lower bunks) are arranged along
walls approximately 36" apart with a center area of 2
rows of single bunks (at this institution the wheelchair

1

COVID-19

RODERICK RICHARDSON

On May 18, 2020, I lost my father, Herman Richardson, after an amputation surgery that me and my sister Herneisha basically talked him into getting. Diabetes had gangrene taking over his legs. I heard he was in so much pain that maybe he was getting four hours of sleep a day.

The doctor said his chances were 50-50. The operation was a success. He was moved from the hospital to rehab, where he was not allowed any visitors. Within two weeks he stopped eating, and on May 18th, COVID-19 claimed another victim. And me, his oldest child, never got a chance to say goodbye.

In here, quarantine started 28 days ago, even though we were told it would be just 14. No one comes around and tells us nothing, the administration is invincible, not a whisper or a peep. Our information comes from inmate.com...lies upon lies. I see stretchers taking inmates out like a silent ambulance. After a few days, I hear nothing about them anymore.

I guess that's what keeps me with hope, the not knowing keeps me fighting to see another day.

In here, there is no such thing as social distance; our masks are made out of the blue cloth we wear, our room-mates sleep three feet overhead and a 12×10-foot cell is our bathroom, kitchen, and living room combined into one.

In here, peanut butter and a half spoon of jelly is served almost every day; if it's not peanut butter, it's watery, slimy, no-tasting baloney. The showers are ice-cold.

Officers come to work angry — most of them don't want
to work. They let the food sit in the hallway until it
gets cold, even though we are only getting one supposed-
to-be-hot meal a day.

My story is the same story of many young Black men
blinded by the reality of life. Dropping out of school to
provide for their mom and siblings, just so the family
can survive.

I've been slave #xxxxxx so long, I feel chains rattle
inside.

For 28 years, seven months, and three days today, I hav-
en't found a way back home.

And now I'm wondering if COVID-19 might be the judge
that sets me free.

IT
WAS
THE
SINKING
SUN
THAT
MADE
ME
REALIZE
HOW
LONELY
I HAD
BECOME

$\longrightarrow$

JOURNEY THROUGH COVID

JOSEPH LIVINGSTON

February 5, 2020 I was transferred from Everglades C.I.
to the Regional Medical Center West Unit in Lake Butler,
Florida, to see an orthopedic specialist. COVID-19 was
just starting to be talked about. Everyone seemed to be
scrambling to understand the virus.

I read everything I could that contained information
about the virus, watching both local and world news daily.
I saw how people in society were horrified of contract-
ing the virus. The staff at RMC West Unit Lake Butler
seemed unconcerned. They continued to not wear face coverings. No one knew who had or didn't have the virus at
Lake Butler since no testing had been done. Lake Butler
is a facility with a very high volume of daily movements,
where safety precautions should be exercised vigorously
due to the facility's many functions.

People were being hospitalized, deaths were mounting.
Inmates still sat four to a table during feeding, and
staff commingled with colleagues and inmates daily.

March 12 a few minutes before 8 a.m., the captain
entered the dorm and announced that visitation was can-
celed until further notice due to the possibility of the
coronavirus being brought into the prisons by visitors.
However, inmates were still being transferred in and out
of the facility, and no face coverings were being worn
by staff and inmates.

March 13 the CDC posted that the coronavirus could survive on plastic or cardboard surfaces for 72 hours. I
was afraid of the surfaces I touched. My conversations

were limited; I isolated as much as I could, and watched my distance when socializing with others.

March 16 movements at Lake Butler were limited to call-outs to the main unit.

March 25 inmates at LBWU began sitting two to a table. On this same date, two inmates at Marion C.I. were diagnosed with the coronavirus.

April 1 sheet day at the West Unit; I turned in my sheets, pillowcase, towel, and washcloth, but only got my sheets back.

April 2 the nurses visited the dorms early in the morning checking inmates for symptoms.

April 8 transporting at Lake Butler resumed, however, no testing was done on inmates, before or after transporting was halted.

April 9 I was told to turn in my blanket; it would be washed every Thursday.

April 14 bang! On my way to breakfast during shift change, I noticed that every officer who entered the facility had a face covering on. A handwashing station was also erected today at the entrance of the dining hall. It was posted two days late.

April 15 the colonel announced that inmates sleep head-to-toe to prevent breathing in each others' faces while sleeping. Two inmates at Black Water Correctional Facility died from the virus.

April 16 I was issued two face coverings constructed from the same material as my uniform. I was told I had to wear a face covering every time I left my bunk and when I exited the dorm.

April 19 none of the officers assigned to the dining hall were wearing face coverings, yet they demanded that inmates wear theirs.

April 22 inmates were told to turn in their face coverings to be tagged and they would be washed every Thursday.

April 23 we were called for breakfast unusually early. When I exited the dormitory, I was told to look down at the pavement, locate a red line and stand on it. The red markings indicated a six-foot interval between each inmate.

May 6 I returned to Everglades C.I. There was no movement but a very high volume of new officers on the compound. I was processed in and assigned housing in B-dorm, bottom floor. Some facets of operations were still in place, but in a very limited way and with new rules: no commingling of inmates from different dorms; inmates were segregated on the recreation yard; inmates were allowed to take showers anytime they wished except at count time; canteen was run by dorm, one pod at a time.

Officers walked around the compound without face coverings or had them hanging under their chins, while demanding inmates wear theirs properly.

May 13 nurses began making rounds to the dorms checking for inmates who exhibited coronavirus symptoms. Despite restrictions in place, individuals from different dorms were still allowed to sit and eat with each other during feeding.

May 25 new face coverings were issued to all inmates at ECI to replace the hastily constructed ones issued. Two inmates who were previously admitted into the clinic with symptoms one week earlier tested positive for the coronavirus. This event caused the medical orderlies to be placed on quarantine.

May 29 Coronavirus testing started at ECI.

○

IF MY
HEADPHONES
AREN'T
BUMPING
MY
MUSIC
FULL BLAST,
I'LL BE
FORCED
TO
LISTEN
TO THESE
CONSTANT
TIRADES
ALL DAY.
THANK GOD
FOR
TAYLOR
SWIFT.

→

SOCIAL DEPRIVATION

LANCE E. PALERMO

The shrill of the sergeant's voice shouted across
the dorm. Social distancing would not only be implemented but strongly enforced by the Texas Department of
Criminal Justice (TDCJ). A minimum of six feet between
inmates at all times; one inmate per table in the chow
hall; ten inmates in the day room at one time.

Personal space is a luxury of the free world. In every
situation, the policy always seemed to get as many
inmates into one place as soon as possible — outside
recreation, the chow hall, taking a shower. All places
were always crammed and overrun with inmates.

For a long time I believed the official TDCJ motto was,
"Pack'em in, common, tighten up, if it ain't touching,
it ain't nothing." But this sergeant explained how all
of these crowded situations were being eradicated. I
sat confused on my bunk, wondering just how much truth
was behind all of these new procedures. In prison there
is a saying, "Don't believe anything you hear, and only
half of what you see." I was skeptical. I was being told
things that I had often wished for, but knew could never
be a reality.

The next morning I proceeded with my usual routine —
brushed my teeth and prepared for work — and walked
toward the "turn out" line, where I would be checked
and rostered for work, then permitted to leave and continue to my assigned work area. But something strange
happened. A guard rapidly approached and yelled, "Six
feet inmates, give yourselves some space." I could not
believe my ears: it was true. Social distancing would
now be enforced.

Work seemed to drag on that day. I wanted the day to
be over so I could see what other changes were being
enforced.

After I was checked back in from work, I proceeded to
the Chow Hall — only one inmate per table; no crowd-
ing, plenty of space for my arms, legs, and tray. It was
quiet. My mind raced to all the times I had been sub-
jected to eating with inmates I was not familiar with,
listening to their meaningless chatter, listening to
them scream across the table or watching another chew
his food with his mouth open. I ate my entire meal with
a smile on my face.

That same night, the day room looked like a ghost town.
Usually it was packed this time of night. There was no
one around. I had an entire bench to myself! I stretched
out my arms and my legs and watched an entire movie
without interruption — no idle talking, no yelling. Not
once did I hear a slamming domino. I was walking on
air, a little slice of heaven in prison.

Days turned into weeks. All surfaces were sprayed with
bleach water and all inmates and staff were required
to wear masks. TDCJ created a safety video for inmates
to watch, illustrating the dangers of COVID-19. I could
recite the video by heart, having had to watch it so
many times.

Visitation was cancelled, along with church services, and
school or any form of academia. The only people coming in
and out of the prison were TDCJ employees. The only outside communication available was from the news stations.

I have often felt that prison is the loneliest place in the world, but you are never alone. Being surrounded by a community of inmates numbs the pain of being separated from family and friends. Being isolated from that community changes the paradigm. I had always heard the expression, "You come into prison alone, you will leave prison alone."

These words seemed so true, and never before had I fixated on the word *alone*.

Meal after meal, I ate from afar. Movie after movie, I watched in silence. More times than not I'd sit down and feel the wet, slimy residue of recently sprayed bleach water. Time after time I heard, "Put on that mask, Inmate!" I asked someone to pass the salt, only to remember there was no one there. I laughed at a comical part of the movie, then looked around to see if anyone else had enjoyed the hilarity, only to be reminded once again that I was alone. I walked to the recreation yard to socialize, only to be disappointed. When I finally could socialize with another inmate, I was promptly reminded, "Six feet, Inmate, give yourselves some space."

I walked outside to witness the sunset, certain that someone else would be out there watching it too. It was the sinking sun that made me realize how lonely I had become.

THE NEW NORMAL

GUSTAVO GUERRA

So what dreams does a lifer have? You know, the regular ones. Eating a medium-rare steak with an ice cold beer. Waking up on a pillow-top mattress. Feeling the lapping water of the ocean on my feet as my toes slowly sink into the wet sand. But that's just the surface.

I also dream of standing on a stage telling people about my redemption and about those still behind the wire. I dream of mentoring at-risk youth and showing them a different way. I dream of book signings and using that platform to address the overlooked issue of mass incarceration. And I dream of returning to prisons as a visitor and encouraging the men to strive for more.

Then I focus on the toilet and the sink right next to it and those dreams disperse behind my reality, streaming down my face as I come to terms with the fact that I will probably never be released from prison. In Florida, life means life.

It is a typical Monday at Everglades Correctional Institution in Florida. Well, typical considering there is a global pandemic. Typical in the sense of face masks, social distancing, and cracked fissures in your hands from washing them so many times.

I wake up about 8:30 after a fitful night's sleep. The heat kept me tossing and turning until I finally passed out — the same heat that wakes me up. The humidity has already begun to batter my sanity.

Breakfast was at 4:45 and I slept right through it. Sleep is the prisoner's refuge — she envelops him in her warm embrace and shelters him from the painful memories and regrets of the waking hours.

I make a strong cup of instant Colombian coffee and grab my folder of assignments. I snag a seat at one of two metal picnic tables in our dorm. They have been painted and repainted several times, as evidenced by the multi-hued chips peeling off the rusted holes. To write, it's important to snatch a seat without a lot of that rust.

I sit down, armed with caffeine and a pen, and take in my surroundings. About twenty guys are out and about. Most of them are clustered on the four metal benches facing the television on the wall. But the DirectTV-fed flat screen television doesn't interest them, rather it's the two industrial oscillating fans mounted on the same wall.

Mornings are the only time I have at the table. The one I am sitting at gets taken over by dominoes and pinochle players after the noon count. The other table is used as spillover for T.V. viewing and fan consumption.

Count is called a little after 11:00. We get locked in our 8×10 cells while security confirms everyone is ac-counted for. The temperature is in the low 90s. My win-dow is broken and I only have a three-inch slat where air is strong-armed by the two extractors on the oth-er side of my cell door. I use sporks to pin a piece of clear plastic to my window to direct the flow of air toward my bunk — a chaingang AC. It makes being locked in bearable.

I pick up an adventure novel for count. I read to dis-tract myself. Otherwise my mind drifts like an unteth-ered balloon. I fantasize about what I will do if I ever get out: I visualize my first meal; I decorate my apartment; I even buy a new wardrobe. Other times, the darkness seeps in and my thoughts turn to all of my mistakes, the people I've hurt, and the realities of my life sentence. It's safer to read.

After count, we head to lunch. We have to exit the dorm in class A uniform, which consists of a blue polyester shirt and pants, white undershirt, socks and shoes.

Meal times take longer now that security is keeping us isolated. There are eight dorms on the compound; 31 separate wings or quads, seven on quarantine. A couple of those are medical isolation for COVID-19 positive cases. At one point we had 14 or 15 wings on quarantine. My wing has remained corona-free since the beginning. It has been a blessing.

Security calls out one wing at a time to feed. This process sometimes takes hours. So, if my dorm is the last one called, it will have been 11 hours since our last meal. To say that people are hangry is an understatement.

It's been four months of being called last almost EVERY day. Four months of the same routine. Four months of looking at the same 64 people. Four months of listening to the same people complain and whine and bitch. These frustrations surface like angry bubbles in a boiling pot of water.

On this day, it is as palatable as the humidity. I try to ignore everything but notice another argument has sprouted. This time about the T.V. Sixty-four people. More than two-hundred channels. And one remote — a recipe for hostility.

We finally head to chow. We are the last wing of the last dorm. We grab our tray from a small rectangular hole in the wall and sit down — two to a table for social distancing, even though we live together. Our food is cold. Of course it is. It was cooked five hours ago. By the time we get back to the dorm, the officers are yelling at us to go to our cells. It's count time again. The evening is a repetition of the afternoon. Same faces. Same arguments. Same expectations for dinner. Then it's count time again. We are released an hour later and I go back to my seat on the bench in front of the fan and Luis sits next to me. I groan. He's one of the more vocal complainers. They've put on a movie we've watched half a dozen times and, sure enough, Luis starts to murmur. I bite my tongue. It's hot and it's been a long day. I don't want to hear his crap but I don't want to move either because I'm in a good spot for the fan.

The old me wants to tell him off and get him mad enough to want to fight. I could use the physical release of aggression. Instead, I play it out in my head. I will probably hurt him. If he needs medical attention, I will go to solitary confinement and end up being transferred when the lockdown lifts. Transferring means losing everything I have worked so hard to achieve. I don't want to be that person anymore. So I turn to Luis.

I ask him why he's so negative all the time. He confesses to allowing the lockdown to get to him. He is worried about his family and misses his chapel programs and services. I explain that I also feel this way. I tell him about all of the programs in which I've been involved. How I was running full tilt prior to the lockdown. How I'm at a dead stop now. How depressed I sometimes get. But I tell him how I get through it. How writing about it helps me vent. And how encouraging others gets us outside ourselves and gives us purpose. And purpose, I emphasize, is what we all desperately need right now.

The amazing part is, he says that I'm right. It's like the heavens have opened up with a choir of angels singing hallelujah. The movie is forgotten — along with the heat and the complainers. By the end, we're both laughing.

I lie on my bunk a short while later. I thank God for self-control. And for the wisdom to see someone else in pain. And even though it is still warm, and even though I still have a piece of plastic on my window directing air on my body, I rest well, ready for another day.

Excerpt from:

ON THE INSIDE LOOKING OUT

CORY PRIDE

My nights were usually haunted by COVID-terrors, an alternation of tossing and turning, and cat naps. This morning though, it was the whirring of power tools that prevented me from a good doze. I attempted, unsuccessfully, to drown out the racket with my pancake-thin pillow, but was forced to crawl from my bunk, grab my binoculars, and make my way to the window. Workers were busy converting hotels into temporary hospitals to help with the surge of hospitalizations. Not far from that, there were dozens of cars lined up at food banks; some lines stretched for two miles. The effect of the virus had quickly taken its toll on the American people, and thousands were searching for what they needed to feed their families. I saw dairy farmers pouring thousands of gallons of milk down drains, and other farmers disposing of thousands of pounds of vegetables. How is it that close to 120,000 people in Missouri are visiting food banks every week, but farmers are throwing tons of food away?

A beautiful pair of Imperial Yellow-winged goldfinches landed on my sill. I looked away from the majestic creatures just in time to see a B-2 bomber and the Blue Angels flying over a hospital to honor our heroes on the front lines of this battle. There were signs high above many restaurants advertising that they were providing free meals for our beloved medical workers. Signs in front of daycares were pledging free childcare to essential workers.

*****

I got up at 4:30am and slipped to the restroom. It was thirty minutes before we were permitted to use the restroom for anything other than relieving our bowels, but I needed to avoid the crowd. I wondered what the parole board would say if I got a conduct violation for this? Did it even matter to them that I had to break institution rules in order to social distance — in order to avoid potentially catching the deadly virus?

BROKEN TILES

EMILIO FERNANDEZ

$E_1M_3P_3T_1Y_4$ yields 32 points at the start of any game. Today it describes the seat across from me, the Scrabble board on the table, and the state of my heart. The empty seat was usually filled by my best friend Joe. We'd spend hours of our prison sentence placing square wooden tiles upon a colorful cardboard battlefield, using Q's and Z's on triple-pointed spaces as Cheshire smiles spread across our faces. But the greatest joy was picking a blank 'wild' tile out of the red velvet bag, our eyes lighting up as we'd bounce it onto the table, saying it was broken because it had no letter, or holding it up to our eyes like a looking glass.

$C_3O_1V_4I_1D_2$ provides 19 points if, and only if, the V is placed on a triple-letter tile and the rest on regular tiles. I wouldn't be surprised if it was added to the next edition of the Scrabble dictionary. It has amassed both fame and death and has made the headline of every news program over the last few months. It was always something distant until the end of May when it arrived in D-Dorm at Everglades C.I. and contaminated over 20 individuals in a single day. Even after being quarantined and locked within an 8×12 two-man cell for 29 days in June, the reality of the virus still did not penetrate my defenses. That is until last week when it took my best friend Joe's life.

$Y_4A_1N_1K_5E_1E_1S_1$, a word that would score 50 individual points for using all seven tiles, was priceless to Joe. It stood for his passion, joy, and heartbreak. He bled pinstripes. Such was his love for them that he contaminated me, a perennial hater of the Evil Empire, to root for them as my American League team. He had listened to every game of theirs for the last 27 years, preferring to hear them over the AM airwaves than watch them in living color. He was with them through all the tiles in the 90s and 2000s, and ever faithful through their only World Series Title-less decade from 2010-2019. And because this season was delayed by the same virus that took his life, he never got to hear Opening Day 2020.

$W_4 I_1 T_1 H_4 O_1 U_1 T_1$ him, prison, Scrabble, and crossword puzzles will never be the same. He won't be there to finish the few words I miss along vertical and horizontal blocks, teaching me what they are so that I know them next time. He won't get to take his granddaughter to Disney and spoil her, buying everything she wanted. He won't get to see his parents' native Italy. No seven-letter banger or blank wild tile will ever evoke the joy it used to. No, not until I get to play with him again upon a Scrabble board made of gold set on a table made of glass with tiles of precious stones. There, our hearts will be unbroken. Actually, the only broken things will be those 'wild' tiles as we bounce them gently on the table with a twinkle in our eyes and a smile on our faces.

Broken Tiles

$E_1 M_3 P_3 T_1 Y_4$ yields 32 points at the start of any game. Today it describes the seat across from me, the Scrabble board on the table, and the state of my heart. The empty seat was usually filled by my best friend Joe. We'd spend hours of our prison sentence placing square wooden tiles upon a colorful cardboard battlefield, using Q_{10}'s and Z_{10}'s on triple-pointed spaces as chesire smiles spread across our faces. But the greatest joy was picking a blank 'wild' tile out of the red velvet bag. Our eyes lighting up as we'd bounce it onto the table saying it was broken because it had no letter or holding up to our eye like a looking glass.

$C_3 O_1 V_4 I_1 D_2$ provides 19 points if, and only if, the V_4 is placed on a triple-letter tile and the rest on regular tiles. I wouldn't be surprised if it was added to the next edition of the Scrabble dictionary. It has amassed both fame and death, and has made the headline of every news program over the last few months. It was always something distant until the end of May when it arrived in D-Dorm at Everglades C.I. and contaminated over 20 individuals in a single day. Even after being quarantined and locked within an 8' x 12' two-man cell for 29 days in June, the reality of the virus still did not penetrate my defenses. That is until last week when it took my best friend Joe's life.

$Y_4 A_1 N_1 K_5 E_1 E_1 S_1$, a word that would score 50 additional points for using all seven tiles, was priceless to Joe. It stood for his passion, joy, and heartbreak. He bled pinstripes. Such was his love for them that he contaminated me, a perennial hater of the Evil Empire, to root for them as my American League team. He had listened to every game of theirs for the last 27 years, preferring to hear them over the AM airwaves than watch them in living color. He was with them through all the tiles in the 90's and 2000's, and ever faithful through their only World Series Title-less decade from 2010-2019. And because this season was delayed by the same virus that took his life, he never got to hear Opening Day in 2020.

W₄ I, T, H₄ O, U, T, him, prison, Scrabble, and crossword puzzles will never be the same. He won't be there to finish the few words I miss along the vertical and horizontal blocks, teaching me what they are so that I know them next time. He won't get to take his granddaughter to Disney and spoil her, buying everything she wanted. He won't get to see his parents' native Italy. No seven letter banger or blank 'wild' tile will ever evoke the joy it used to. No, not until I get to play with him again upon a Scrabble board made of gold set on a table made of glass with tiles of precious stones. There, our hearts will be unbroken. Actually, the only broken things will be those 'wild' tiles as we bounce them gently on the table with a twinkle in our eyes and a smile on our faces.

This piece was written in response to hearing that my best friend Joe had passed away on July 15, 2020 due to complications from Covid-19.

"

SO, JUST KEEP THAT IN MIND THE NEXT TIME YOU DECIDE TO PULL YOUR GUN OUT AND AIM;

JOHNNY LEE HILL

WE REALLY AREN'T THAT DIFFERENT, THE WAY YOU ENTERED INTO THE WORLD, IS THE SAME WAY I CAME...

"

I CAN'T BREATHE

HELENA L. PAYNE

In Memory of George Floyd
Black Lives Matter

I feel like the world is on my shoulders
Hot coals and heavy boulders
The pain is getting stronger
All I can see is my mother and my daughter
I once was young, but now I'm older
The world is getting colder
I'll be home, is what I told her
Surrounded by police
Black clouds, it seemed to me
Spare me the knee
Home is what's free to me
Please help me
A Black child
Survival is in me
I demand to stand on my feet
And be treated like a human being
Don't take my life away from me

UNTITLED

ISRAEL (IZZY) MARTINEZ

When I watch the news and see another man not far from my own pigment of color get a size 10 steel-toe boot pressed against his cheek, I feel some kind of way. And then the media showcases the circus act of COVID-19. This is the great equalizer, the thing to change the political worldview to something else other than the oppression of a people, the normal working-class American, that Black man across the street who says good morning to you every day and is just trying to make ends meet. Corona says he doesn't matter, that he is just another statistic.

This world is full of regrets, and I am one of them.

The DOC will not lift its boot off my own neck. I haven't breathed properly in almost a decade. People focus on the corruption between two political parties rather than the systematic racism happening in the justice system. 'Cause that is the 'New Normal.'

But all that's hearsay and that wouldn't hold up in court. Just like the idea of a #PrisonLivesMatter movement. If they have no problem killing everyday Americans on the street, what chance do we have?

Then the T.V. turns off and that reminds me, our lives don't matter and hashtags resemble prison bars. So forgive me if I don't put my hands up these days.

WE ARE THE SAME

JOHNNY LEE HILL

I have a heart that beats;
I have breath that goes into my lungs.
I have blood that flows through my veins;
I have a soul...
don't you have one?

Then, why do you hate me so,
and treat me as if my life matters none?
Why do you insist on murdering
our brothers, sisters...
fathers and sons?

Do I not LOVE like you?
Or shed blood like you do?
Do I not have feelings, as well?
I enjoy kisses and hugs, too.

I have three beautiful kids and an amazing mom;
come on, I'll even show you.
But that can only happen if you take the time
to get to know me
and I get to know you.

All in all, I hurt like you
and I, too, can feel pain.
We may have come from different neighborhoods
with different backgrounds and different skin colors,
but we are very much the same.

So, just keep that in mind
the next time you decide to pull your gun out and aim;
we really aren't that different,

the way you entered into the world,
is the same way I came...

"We Are The Same"

I have a heart that beats; I have breath that goes into my lungs. I have blood that flows through my veins; I have a soul... don't you have one? Then, why do you hate me so, and treat me as if my life matters none? Why do you insist on murdering our brothers, sisters... fathers and sons?

Do I not LOVE like you? Or, shed blood like you do? Do I not have feelings, as well? I enjoy kisses and hugs, too. I have 3 beautiful kids and an amazing Mom; come on, I'll even show you. But, that can only happen, if you take the time to get to know me and I get to know you.

All-in-all, I hurt like you and, I too, can feel pain. We may have come from different neighborhoods, with different backgrounds and different skin colors, but, we are very much the same. So, just keep that in mind, the next time you decide to pull your gun out and aim, ~~we~~ really aren't that different; the way you entered into the world, is the same way I came....

Poem, written and created by:
Johnny Lee Hill, ████████████
an inmate in the Florida Department of Corrections;

████████████████████████████

Rest In Peace, George
Floyd!!!

A BREATHING TRIBUTE

PIERRE PINSEN

A Black man's tears are the proverbial tree that falls in the forest. Those who believe that we don't cry because of hypermasculinity have no idea what it means to be a Black man in America.

Pain is our inheritance, vulnerability — a feeling, and being endangered is a realization. I had been in George Floyd's position a number of times before I was the age of 15. I thought that a knee on my back was standard operating procedure, that I was born to supply the neck as a resting place for oppression. Strange fruit not only dangles from trees, it also falls onto street tops or is crushed beneath boots. No one cries over spilled fruit.

This year I have witnessed Black men crying — on television. I wondered what gave them the audacity to be human? Their tears make me afraid. Black men aren't supposed to cry. If we are all crying, who is keeping watch? COVID-19 has helped many of these Black men recognize their vulnerability. Police brutality has helped to reveal that they are endangered. I am a tree that fell in the woods. No one was around. I needed a moment, so I stole it like I had no right to it. Tears subsided and I inhaled deeply. There I was, breathing and crying — two things Black men aren't supposed to do.

AM I SPEAKING HEBREW?

CHRISTOPHER MALEC

We, are a culture
an isolated peoples
Hebrews under Pharaohs
In a neo-Auschwitz, forgotten
Hungrier than a heartbeat
On the cusp of love
The only exodus
That stays in place
When I die
Use my ribs as piano keys
To tap the music I left
And hear Justice played
A sycophantic orchestra of wounded promises sobbing,
Abandonment screaming arias of reconcile,
Amplified off the trashcans in alleys of revenge,
And the thumping contractions giving birth to death
Living in the nightmarish shadow
Of an oppressor's dream, some
Other brothers of mine have
Tilled this field longer than I
A shame Nat couldn't resurrect in a vessel
Emptying its own into a joint rolled with Spice
As I wonder if this country's a factory for synthetic souls
And we, the defects
Rejects in the mill of a contemporary
1984 Big Brother becoming real
For Orwellian pigs to eat the last
Of democracy's latest litter
Clipped the wings off everything
And everyone capable of flight
So Jim C's contrast
Didn't seem so stark against the dark
Irony is not teaching

Distinction of class
In classes on the lower
Echelons of tax brackets
Beginning authoritarian bend of will early on
So when the impoverished wheel of destiny
Falls flat on its side
The spokes trap 'em in place
We just don't see how
To climb through these bars
Fashioned especially for us
Since we played on monkey bars
We haven't counted for every overseer
There are fifty of us to match and that
This plantation is simply fenced in
A concentrated camp of Stockholm
See, justice without a criminal
Is like Christianity without Jesus
Because every righteousness
Needs a fall guy
And every emperor needs a threat
To protect his people from
Whether it exists
Or not
But every oppression needs a Moses
A chosen, who speaks redemption
Shifts tensions back the ones stretching
Similarities into differences among the victims
Are you one of the ones who thinks
That a few scattered, whispered doubts
Travels way further
Than a thousand synchronized, reassuring shouts
Revolution
Is music
Composed in notes strummed on the phone lines of streets
without power,
While single mothers crash stop signs together like cymbals
In front of courtrooms performing post-legacy abortions on
Future children echoing crescendos through halls in
schools of law

Let the bass of your contempt
Shake the branches of government
'Til the rotted apples fall and the roots
Of discrimination die
There is power
In hunger

PIERRE PINSEN

I
THOUGHT
THAT
I
WAS
BORN
TO
SUPPLY
THE
NECK
AS
A
RESTING
PLACE
FOR
OPPRESSION

→

GONE TOO SOON

BIG MAC

Hey baby girl.

Hey Daddy.

Can Daddy talk to you for a sec? Princess, in two more days you will be 13 years old; what do you want to be when you grow up?

Daddy, I want to be a doctor because I want to help people when they are hurting.

That's good Tasha, but in order for you to achieve this goal, you have to stay in school.

I will, I plan on being the first to graduate from college.

Stay focused, Princess.

Oh, I will Daddy and I am. Can I go over to Tranes' house so we can get ready for my birthday party you're throwing for me?

Yeah, Princess, go ahead. Be safe.

Hezekiah!

Yeah, Ma!

Boy, come on in here and help me do these dishes.

Ma — the dishes, that's girl stuff, why can't you get Tisha?

Boy, you heard what I said, if I wanted to call Tisha, then I would have, but I called Hezekiah.

Okay, Ma, at your service. What's up?

Nothing, I just wanna spend some time with my baby, is that alright? Can a mother do that?

Yeah Ma, but doing the dishes...?

Oh boy, shut up and dry the dishes off with that towel while I wash them and rinse them. Hezekiah? Let me ask you a question. You're about to graduate from high school, and I was just wondering what are your plans after you graduate? Do you have any?

Yeah Ma, I have plans. My first plan was to play football, but that's the easy way out for a project kid. Then I thought about being a lawyer because when I look at how Black people are misrepresented it does something to me, and I want to help. I also thought that once football is over, then what? I want to show my friends, and the kids in these projects, whether it be the Beans, PSU, Lincoln Field, the Blackblues, the Graveyard, or Lodgemont, I want to show them that football is not the only way out. Ma, what are you crying for?

Because your momma is so proud of your determination; you must have gotten that from my side of the family.

Yeah, I guess I did, Ma. Can you take me to visit my old boy the weekend after I graduate?

Yeah, I got you, baby. Well, we all done here.

Okay, Momma. I'm about to walk down to the Square and play some chess with the old heads.

Okay baby, be careful.

Always Ma, love you lady.

> Look here, Playah, you want to be a part of this family, you want the respect and fear that comes along with being in this family? You want the finer things in life that comes with being in this family?

> Yeah, Brah, I want all that, just tell me what I gotta do.

> Playah, you gotta catch a body, you gotta prove that you got heart for this.

> A body?

> Yep, a body. And listen, I don't care who it is, it could be somebody's grandma, grandpa, momma, daddy, sister, or brother, daughter or son, it don't matter just prove your worth, get that body.

> Cool, let's do this.

> Check it, I heard there was a party going on over there behind Here's Help, in the little residential neighborhood, that's where you catch your first body.

> You got some fire?

> Kiah, dawg. I ain't got none.

Well, don't worry about it, reach in the back and pull that draco from back there. You know how to make it spit?

Hell yeah, Playah. Just watch me in action.

Cool, let's get your first body then.

Hey Kiah.

What's up Ghost?

I got a spot at the chess table for us.

You ready for your daily beat down? Ghost, do you really think that I'm going to let you checkmate like that?

Hey, Ward.

Yeah?

Who you like, Ghost or me?

Listen young fella, call me Bennet. I ain't in it when you gone off to college, I gotta be stuck with this one. One thing about you, Ward, you're smart. Oh Lord, here comes trouble.

What's up Old School?

What's up, Crazy?

Hey, you seen that boy Rat lately?

Who are you to be asking about my uncle Rat?

Dude owe me a guap and I want that.

Yeah, you'll get it when he's got it.

What are you, his mouthpiece?

I ain't his mouthpiece, but while he ain't here I'm gonna speak up for him.

What's your name?

They call me Kiah.

Well, listen Kiah, I advise you to stay in your place, don't funk out of bounce.

You the one coming around here asking questions like you the po-po.

Slow your roll jit, you don't know who you messing with. Ghost, Ward, get your little protégé.

Come on, Kiah, let's get back to playing chess.

Yeah, Kiah, get back to playing chess because what I'm trying to give your uncle, you can get it instead, don't matter to me.

>	Damn, they thick out here, it's a damn shame the grim reaper is about to spoil the fun.

>	You ready, Playah?

>	Hell yeah.

>	When I pull up in front of the house, let loose on them. Now, fool.

>	*Dat. Dat. DDDDDDD, dat. Dat. dat.*
>	*(Tires screeching.) (Screams everywhere.)*

>	What the...

Where my baby at? Oh Lord, don't let her be out there. Princess? Princess? Tasha? Tasha? Tasha? Where are you? Oh, no no no no no! Tasha, look at me baby. Look at Daddy.

Daddy, it burns. Help me, Daddy. I don't want to die. I want to be a doctor, Daddy.

Daddy ain't going to let you die. Can somebody call the police? I got you, baby.

Daddy?

Yes, Princess?

I see Mommy.

No, no, no, you don't see Mommy. Look at me, Princess, it's going to be alright.

Daddy, I'm tired, I want to go to sleep.

Stay with me, Princess. Stay with me.

Daddy, I'm cold. Hold me, Daddy.

I got you, Princess.

Goodnight, Daddy.

Princess, Princess. No, God, no.
(uncontrollable sobbing.)

Darryl, Darryl come on baby, she's gone. Come on.
(More uncontrollable sobbing.)

This young ***** just don't know what he done got him-self into, since he's Rat's nephew, he's going to get what's meant for Rat.

Hey Kiah..

Who that?

It's Crazy, fool, give this to your uncle Rat for me.

Datka, daka, daka, daka.

Straight drop, fool. Let's get out of here.

Where that boy Kiah at, he should be home by now.

    (Tisha bursts through the door crying)

    Ma, they killed Kiah, they killed him Ma.

    Kiah, my Kiah. He's going to be coming through
    that door any minute.

    Sirens in the background.

    Dee Dee, they killed him.

    Why y'all keep saying that. My baby is not dead.

    *Dee Dee slowly walks outside and sees her son
    lying in the street and she breaks down.*

    Gone too soon.

    Young Lives Matter!

Excerpt from:

THE WORST OF BOTH WORLDS

LEONARD L. PARKER

I never did like sirens
fire trucks looking for fire
paramedics picking up bodies
and the police just looking for anybody
with skin like mine

LEONARD L. PARKER

AND
THE
POLICE
JUST
LOOKING
FOR
ANYBODY
WITH
SKIN LIKE
MINE

→

I CAN'T BREATHE

LAWRENCE DEMERS

I can't breathe, I can't breathe, will forever be sung,
As protesters chant for change to come.
This misuse of power has reached a new height,
This moment in history when day turned to night.

I can't breathe, I can't breathe, those were his words
As he struggled for breath and died by the curb.
A young child's father, a mother's bright son,
He once had a family, now look what they've done.

He can't breathe, he can't breathe, those were the cries,
As the nation watched the light fade from Floyd's eyes.
And no matter what it was they would have you believe,
That cop surely knew that George couldn't breathe.

He can't breathe, he can't breathe, you are killing him!
And when it was over, things grew more grim.
With a knee on his neck, his last living sight,
Was a bystander's screaming, "Man, this ain't right."

I can't breathe, I can't breathe, that's what he said
For nearly nine minutes, and now the man's dead.
Let us never forget this day turned to night,
As we march on together, turning wrong into right.

As we breathe, as we breathe, we will continue this fight.
In Floyd's loving memory, may all races unite.
Just beware the forces that are out to deceive,
That divide us asunder until we can't breathe.

BLACK MAGIC

ANTOINE J. MURPHY

May weather
Feel like June
Feel like December
Recorded live
I seen his eyes
Seen my own
Land of many lakes
Formed another
Justice seems counterfeit
Who U R
Who U wit
What crime did U commit?
Black lives
Seem counterfeit
When
Those sworn 2 serve-n-protect
Got da nerve
2 "perve-n-neglect"
Rodney King. No respect
9 minutes!
Police brutality
Crucifixion mentality
Jesus couldn't breathe
Black lives matter?
Only on a T
Worn by a Negro
German Shepherd.

BLACK MAGIC

~~[scribbled out]~~ June 27, 2020   by Antoine J. Murphy

May weather
feel like June
feel like December
cryEE eyed tissue
we remember
George Floyd
Cotton pick'n mouth
"I can't breathe"
barely exclaimed
on his belly resistance was claimed
recorded live
I seen his eyes
seen my own
land of many lakes
formed another
justice seems counterfeit
who U R
who U wit
what crime did U commit?
black lives, seem counterfeit
when
those sworn 2 "serve -n- protect"
got da nerve
2 "perve -n- neglect"
Rodney King No respect
9 minutes!
made in God's image
it is finished

Police brutality
crucifixions mentality
Jesus couldn't breathe
black lives matter?
                    Only on a T
worn by a Negro
German Shepherd. Named: "here boy"

THE MURDER OF GEORGE FLOYD

HOWARD OVERTURF

No wonder so many Americans protest
The murder of George Floyd
Has opened America's eyes
I hope those officers fry
Look what happened to Breonna Taylor
The police tried to cover it up
Because they are so corrupt
The prison system is the same
They kill inmates and have no shame
You won't see it in the news
But the Feds come in and bust a few
I guess that's all they can do
Nurses help to cover it up
I've seen them beat an inmate in cuffs
And they think they are so tough
Cowards if you ask me
Lock them up and throw away the key
Some officers think they are above the law
From what I saw
America has had enough
It's about time you wear some cuffs
We will see how tough you are
Once you are behind bars

Excerpt from:

CAN'T BREATHE

ZAZA RIVERA

A steady drum and beat that continues to throb us even in our sleep, while men struggle to breathe under the keen eyes of nurses and doctors, hooked up to machines and ventilators; men on the street take their last breath under the knees of uniformed gang members.

But what is really making us choke? What's really cutting our air circulation, and strangling us as human beings on a planet deteriorating from so much hate and biasness?

It is the lack of a system that teaches humility, it is the colonialistic mindset engraved in our psychological imprint. It is the disrespect of culture and differentiation and the judgment of skin color and not character and personality. Instead of focusing on togetherness for the sake of humanity in the face of an unremorseful disease, we allow the most perhaps curable disease to destroy lives, and take them.

Spiritually, we're all losing air.

UNTITLED

MS. ALISHA MICHELLE WARD

Seems we're all frustrated with that COVID-19,
But let's look at some good that it brought to the scene.
Floyd's tragedy would've been another blip in our minds,
If the virus hadn't given us so much idle time.
First we were appalled, then we were sad,
Unconsoled in our grief, and then we got mad.
A movement was born with a legitimate cause,
Black Lives Matter too, please hold your applause.
"My Daddy Changed the World" she said, signing our checks,
Damn shame it was with that honkey's knee on his neck.
Think of this too, when it comes to this disease,
How many of us heathens actually got on our knees?
When you think it's your time all kinds of stuff changes,
Call on Jesus quick when they're talking
funeral arrangements.
Social distancing is another blessing that old 19 brings,
Especially in the morning when your roommate's
breath sings.
Our government paid to put food on every table.
Before the pandemic I'd have said that's a fable.
Before COVID-19 came we were all drifting apart,
But now because they force it, we've had a change of heart.
We have time to reflect on the things that matter most,
Maybe clean out some closets and get rid of some ghosts.
Yeah you can gripe about all that's gone wrong
And you'll probably find a crowd who wants to sing along.
But when you pull off your mask and kiss your loved
one good night,
Take time to thank God for all that's gone right.

Excerpt from:

I WILL BREATHE

AARON "A.J." WRIGHT

I will fight but I won't grieve
Neither shall my folk when it's my time to bleed
'Cause no matter how many times you put your
knife or your bullet in my back
Or your noose of your knee on my neck
Or lock me in a cage and purposely lose the keys
The omnipotent, omniscient fact will remain:
I will breathe!

BLACK IS BEAUTIFUL

MAURICE REED

As the power of my prayer ignites an eternal spark through the pores of my fingertips, I glance at the vast amount of darkness as it swallows my vision. My eagerness for freedom cries to the throne of the most High, thoughts are diverted from the glamorous shine of the night sky, how it reflects what I see every day in the mirror when I say,

Black is Beautiful and How Beautiful is Black.

Goosebumps awake from slumber through my pigment. I shudder at mistakes that led me to an everlasting fall in this dark hole. Every day it's a reminder that my sinful desires have elected to blacken me out. Beneath the sand, pressure on this black coal of a heart has been solidified by agape love, polished and cleansed within mercy and forgiveness of God. Now a diamond, the shine from within has tormented the smut that once covered this dim vessel; without soot this gem could never glimmer. Now I say,

Black is Beautiful and How Beautiful is Black.

The prints of my character have been graffiti. The earth as my canvas has been sprayed by a scabbed intellect that reveals his wounds in due time. Blossom from a black cloud that ruins 11 years of order and instruction has mutated the color of petals of what was a dying rose emerging through cracks from an unfinished road. The melanin of my surface adapts to the harsh conditions every day. Even in the sun, skin cells absorb damage from ultraviolet rays. Grateful I am when I say,

Black is Beautiful and How Beautiful is Black.

JIMMY MURDOCK

"

I BEEN PUSHED OFF HOPE SO MANY TIMES I LEARNED TO LAND WITH NO PARACHUTE

UNTITLED

NIGEL KELLEY

This year has seen many things, but easy or comfortable doesn't come to mind. The months have flown by at a dizzying pace, with adversity as the prevailing theme. I'm currently incarcerated and have been for 16 years. It's hard to describe the experience of incarceration while keeping a proper perspective. As humans we have the ability to adapt to most situations. What may seem mundane to me (a man who's incarcerated) would probably be daunting to the reader.

Imagine undressing in a room with 25 other people for what's called a "strip search." It's like a game of Simon Says, only more serious. You start with the blue shirt, which resembles the top of hospital scrubs. Take it off, turn it upside down, shake it out, throw it on the floor. Then the pants. Take them off, turn them upside down, shake them out, and put them on the floor. Then the white shirt, the socks, and lastly the boxers. Once you're "stripped" you have to open your mouth, run your fingers through your gums, stick your tongue out, then run your fingers through your hair. The last two steps are a little graphic. They have to make sure you don't have anything hidden in your groin area, and last but not least...the coupe de grâce. Turn around, bend at the waist, spread, squat, cough, and lift each foot so the officer can see the bottoms of your feet. To the uninitiated this would be a very degrading experience. I've literally done this hundreds of times, which has turned it into an inconvenience at most.

The questions I've asked myself are: how do I explain my COVID-19 experience to the outside observer and then correlate it to incarceration; and what's taking place

within our country and society? What will the impact
be within corrections and the justice system after this
is all over? Will this pandemic change the way we view
life? Will we adapt to our situation and overcome the
circumstances?

My journey started from the bottom. I came to prison a
young man with a life sentence. This type of sentence
isn't for the faint-hearted. You have to be mentally
strong to endure it. I could embellish my circumstances
and say that I handled it like a "soldier," but I would
only be lying.

I can recall the day I was sentenced. The judge said,
"I have no choice but to sentence you to natural life in
the Florida Department of Corrections." Due to a mandatory sentencing law, the judge was required to give
me the statutory maximum. I knew what my sentence was
going to be a month prior, but his words were still
shocking.

After court, there were six of us on the van going back
to jail. The men were talking about the sentences they'd
received, complaining about three years in prison or
two years probation. I sat in silence, but was ready to
explode. My new reality felt like a yoke around my neck,
full of weight and hardship. I knew that I was going to
be sent to the 'Panhandle' due to the length of my sentence. The 'Panhandle' is in North Florida and is known
for abusive officers and oppressive living conditions.

As these thoughts raced through my mind, I could still
hear these guys in the background complaining and it

only made me feel worse. Finally, someone looked my way and asked, "So, what did they give you?"

This was the first time I'd spoken to anyone since my sentencing a few hours earlier. I looked at him and said "I got life."

That was it, no elaboration, no anger, just the weight of those three words was all that came out.

The banter on the van stopped abruptly; the men were busy reassessing their sentences. Usually words of encouragement are given to minimize the loss that incarceration brings. But it's hard to look at the bright side of a life sentence. The silence implied the finality of my situation. I literally felt ill.

When I got back I went straight to my bunk to lie down. I couldn't bring myself to call home even though I knew my family was hurting worse than me. I'd never felt more ashamed in all my life as I recalled my family's tearful pleas. They knew my sentence was mandatory and still had the courage to testify. I felt like such a failure for the selfish choice I'd made. Sometimes events unfold that leave a mark. This was one of those days; COVID-19 has been another.

COVID-19 hit our planet with little fanfare. It was so far away, and it's hard to understand the contagiousness of something you can't see. We went a few months with no COVID-19 at our institution. We were limited in our movements and had to wear masks but that was like trying to stop a forest fire with a garden hose. Our institution is in Dade County and has been a hot spot since the beginning. The living quarters of prisons are confined by design, making them veritable petri dishes for COVID-19. We use the same phones, showers, and restrooms, basically everything. We're housed in army style barracks (called an open bay dorm) with a lot less space. Once a spark was set off it spread like a wildfire. I won't get into what could have been done better, because it would confuse the purpose of this writing. I can assure you that there's never been a protocol for something like this, so it was new for everyone. COVID-19 is unique because it has such a wide range of severity. One person may be asymptomatic, another may have minor symptoms, while someone else needs hospitalization.

We see violence and death on a regular basis in prison. This was different. Usually when someone is seriously hurt in prison it has a direct correlation to their lifestyle choices. If one chooses to do drugs, an over-dose is possible. If one chooses to be in a gang then getting stabbed is a possibility. COVID-19 doesn't care about your political leanings, religious beliefs, or lifestyle choices. Its simplicity is astonishing. It has one purpose, to find a host and multiply.

My symptoms were minor: headache, slight fever, body aches, and a loss of smell. Not everyone fared as well. We've had multiple hospitalizations, five inmate deaths, and one staff death. I had one personal friend who passed away.

I spent 40 days on quarantine and 21 days in isolation after testing positive for COVID-19. While sitting in a locked cell I had a moment of clarity as the Florida sun beat on my wall. Looking back, I realized I'd been through so much. Six years ago I went back to court and got my life sentence overturned. I thought to myself, had it not been for my life sentence, I wouldn't be the man I am today. Had it not been for the adversity of incarceration, I never would have looked at myself and made the changes necessary for growth.

This situation was just another opportunity to grow and become stronger. The uncertainty that COVID-19 brings makes us fearful of the unknown. Nobody knows what the future holds; we see death every day. It seems endless at times. The comfort of human contact is non-existent. Finances are in the air. As I said earlier, it's hard to explain incarceration. COVID-19 is just like incarceration. The uncertainty you feel in this moment is what millions of men and women have endured for decades. Simply put, COVID-19 and incarceration are cut from the same cloth.

I look at the unrest our country is facing and see it as part of the birth process. I don't know the experience first hand but all the mothers reading this know what I'm talking about. Pregnancy is bittersweet, joyful yet extremely uncomfortable. Once labor starts the pain comes, that's why it's called labor pains. Our country is experiencing labor pains, we're on the verge of a birth. I have faith that power will concede something. Equality can't be a privilege; it must be a right. Our humanity demands it. Flags are falling, and the symbols of oppression are disappearing from plain view. But we must as a society face the oppression that comes cloaked in righteousness. The justice system — from arrest to conviction and incarceration — needs fundamental changes. We cry out not for money or fame, not for power or position. We simply want to be seen. See us for the things that make us human. We're fathers, brothers, and sons. We laugh; we feel pain and loss. We've tasted love, and felt joy. No one should be defined by the worst thing they've done.

We're so much more than that. Indifference is just another link of the chain that keeps us shackled in bondage. Too many men and women have been left in a state of disrepair. If we say we're a nation of equality and fairness, we must have compassion for those who may be struggling, those who are still trying to find their true selves. Give us the tools to become successful, such as trades, substance abuse counseling, and mental health training. Corrections is often overlooked due

to the nature of crime. The issue has become too abso-
lute. Admittedly there are people in prison that have no
intentions of changing, but policy decisions should take
everyone into consideration.

Even with the current state our country is in, I'm still
hopeful for what lies ahead. It may seem like a dark
time now, but light is on the horizon. I see the protests and people standing up for what's right, and I
know a whole generation has been awakened. COVID-19 will
leave a mark on us all, but change requires giving up
something of value for something greater. That's the
definition of sacrifice. Know that the sacrifices we're
all making will be for a better future for our children.
In these trying times make sure to let those you care
about know how important they are. And lastly, be brave,
be kind, and be authentic.

BILLY F. MARTIN III

**TOILET
PAPER
CANNOT
SAVE
YOU**

Excerpt from:

MIRRORING A MASK

<u>CORAL DALY</u>

A woman hides behind her mask. She lifts her head high.
Collections of scars tell stories. The remnants of her
demons. Her daily battle. Weakness or strength, both are
excruciating. You're just a number, bound to years, lost
in the stack of paperwork. Look the part of a convict
– try to look normal. So many years inside have erased
that look they call normal. At least we can legally
wear a mask now. At least I can hide from myself now.
No! Never!

WHO CARES

ANGELA WILLINGHAM

The numbers are climbing higher
My heart is beating quick,
I have but one desire
And that's for me not to get sick.
I seen my friend leave on oxygen
I pray she makes it through,
How can you sit unconcerned
What if it was your family
Or even YOU!
I wasn't sentenced to live in fear
For a low-risk non-violent crime,
I have to pay my debt to society
But I was never sentenced to die.
Where's the compassion, where's the concern
Or should I be added to those already gone.
Could you imagine the stress, the worry, the wait
While watching the news of people - Dying Everyday!
There's no social distancing in prison
No matter how you mask or wash your hands,
The one thing that continuously plagues
Your Mind - That somebody, somewhere, somehow
Will please UNDERSTAND.

I tested positive for the coronavirus on July
22, 2020. And my fellow inmate Saferia Johnson
passed away this morning due to COVID-19.

MY ESCAPE

TRAVIS R. MONN

There's a room with no windows, no peace and no love
A room with no comfort and no one above
There's a light on the ceiling, a lock on the door
And a cold lonely soul lying still on the floor
His dark eyes aren't open, his heart's filled with pain
And his wandering mind is no longer sane
As the coldness grows stronger, he starts to awake
But only to realize his dreams were all fake
His dreams are all lost and will never come true
Now his only escape is the blade in his shoe
His death went unnoticed all through the day
Until his body was found in an ill-mannered way
He was down on the floor, his arms pulled in tight
But only to keep the blood out of sight
His name wasn't mentioned, his family's unknown
Because most of his life he lived all alone
He lived in a cell where his name was a number
And his only pleasures were the things he'd remember

"My Escape"

There's a room with no windows, no peace and no love
a room with no comfort and no one above
there's a light on the ceiling, a lock on the door
and a cold lonely soul lying still on the floor
his dark eye's aren't open, his heart's filled with pain
and his wandering mind is no longer sane.
As the coldness grows stronger he starts to awake
but only to realize his dreams were all fake
his dream's are all lost and will never come true
now his only escape is the blade in his shoe
His death went unnoticed all through the day
until his body was found in an ill-mannered way
he was down on the floor with his arms pulled in tight
but only to keep the blood out of sight
His name wasn't mentioned, his family's unknown
because most of his life he lived all alone
he lived in a cell where his name was a number
and his only pleasures were the things he'd remember.

DISSIDENT

BILLY F. MARTIN III

We watched silently...but that is what we do. We are a silent society that places a high level of value on the ability to remain hidden...and the ability to deflect too much interest or notice.

COVID-19 did not create much fanfare in our world. We believe half of what we see, and none of what we hear. We have heard all manner of sensationalist claims and projections over the years...we have seen the shelves of Publix, Home Depot, and Walmart cleared before. The world hasn't ended yet.

We did think it was rather funny that the biggest commodity this time...was toilet paper. But, to be honest, we think a lot of the things you do are strange and unnecessary.

If you knew the things that we know, you would be much less afraid of losing the pettiest of comforts...and, you would realize that the true "security" is a state of mind that is founded in confidence and faith.

Toilet paper cannot save you.

We have lost everything...even the most basic respect of others...and quite often, of ourselves.

Some of us have been down these roads time and time again...and we have forgotten what it is like to belong to your world. Some of us never knew.

We are soldiers of necessity, often uneducated,
untrained, and undisciplined...we fight a war of no con-
sequence, with no purpose, and no goal.

...And here we sit...
watching...unable to have our voices heard.

LOCKS AND KEYS

DENALI BREHMER

People are always telling me that patience is key. But what use is a key without a lock? Life is a lock with many keys. Each door you open and go through is a memory that makes you who you are and who you will become.

Life has thrown me many keys. Each door has been harder to open than the last. People say it'll always get worse before it gets better. My question is: When will it get better?

Growing up was hard for me. It was always 'Learn fast or be left behind.' I was the second oldest of five kids and had to be a good role model for my siblings. I was adopted at a young age but I've always felt like a charity case.

I have a lot of 'disorders' that make me different and in school I was set apart from the other kids. I didn't want to get bullied more than I already was, so even though I knew the right answer I stayed quiet. I didn't try to apply myself until I was a junior in high school.

Music connects to everyone in some way. It got me through life and all its damned doors. I always took it for granted. So when it got taken away, I fell. Hard.

Drugs can really mess up someone's life. As you get older, people always tell you drugs are bad and to stay away from them. I heard all the talks and speeches. But hearing about how good drugs made you feel and how they took the pain away made me want to try them. That was when I began my downward spiral into the dark.

Being in jail, you get a lot of time to really sit and think. Everything just hits you all at once and you either break down or break through. Prison opened up my eyes to who I had become and what I have been through.

Jail changes you; some change more than others. Some are frequent patrons, others come once and never return. But the few who call this place 'home' are the ones who stayed the same.

I've lost a lot throughout my life. It never was something small for me, it was always something important. I lost my best friends, my family and home. But coming to jail, I've found something more important. I found myself. Friends come and go, family isn't forever, and home is where you make it. But who you truly are is the most important thing you have.

Jail sucks. It really sucks! But I've never felt better. People here, they understand what it is like to never fit in, to lose everything and to not know who you are anymore.

Everyone is in yellow here. No matter the crime, we are all equal. Just because you'll one day be getting out, or are staying here for the rest of your life, doesn't mean that I'm better than you or you're better than me. We both made mistakes to get here. Only difference is, I'm choosing to be the version of myself I want to be.

Just because I've messed up, doesn't mean I'm a bad person. We all break the rules one way or another. We can do so many good things throughout our lives, but we are judged by our last worst act. What right do I have to judge you for your past mistakes when I have my own?

People are scared of differences. They shun the unique and odd. A person is a person, no matter what their stories say. You're the author of your own life story, you can edit all you want. But there always is the rough draft that will stay with you.

The world looks down on us because we have a bad label. Everyone has a bad label, ours is just out in the open. People say be proud and not hide who you are. Yet they keep their labels tucked away.

Criminals are seen as 'damaged goods,' like a can with a dent in it. Most would put the can back on the shelf, but a select few will take it. We might be damaged on the outside, but we are whole on the inside.

It's hard to talk to people you once knew outside the fence. Once you come to jail, you know what it's like to lose your freedom in every way, to have every small liberty taken for granted ripped away. They just don't know.

Being cut off from the world and kept behind a fence would change most people. I used to blame the world for my problems. I blamed everyone else for my mistakes. I lived life like I was some spoiled little rich kid who expected to get everything I wanted. Then I grew up too fast.

All it takes is one moment to change you. These days, people ask if I'm 30 or 35. I feel robbed of my years to just goof off and party like there's no tomorrow. I missed out on so much. It hits close to home. In truth, I'm barely 20 years old, but I act older. Most days, I'm shocked I'm so young, but that just means I have more time to learn and grow.

Prison is a rough road to go down. It's full of potholes, bumps, and rocks. No one said it was a smooth ride. My best advice I can give anyone in jail is to not let your label define you. If you love who you are, then don't change for the sake of someone else.

Life is full of many wonderful things, but it does have its monsters. You never know what's behind the door. Just because you have the key doesn't mean you have to open the door. So my question to you is this:

What doors will you choose to open and which ones will you keep closed?

ARTWORK BY: ANONYMOUS, INCARCERATED IN
FEDERAL PRISON

UNTITLED

DAMIAN BLACK

I have been in San Quentin since November 5th, 2019. Out of all the people here in San Quentin South Block Alpine section, I am almost certain I have been here the longest. I have seen hundreds of people come and go, leaving me behind. My processing was delayed. The month of March was supposed to be the month I would finally leave this terrible place to go to the best prison in all of California. That did not happen. The week I was scheduled to leave is the week transfers stopped and the beginning of our lockdown process started.

Since I arrived in prison, things have always been harder for me compared to most others. Alpine section is for what's called "SNY" inmates — Sensitive Needs Yard. Alpine is where dropout (ex) gang members, people who just chose not to be a part of General Population prison politics, people with cases involving child endangerment, sex offenders, and snitches, are housed for reception in San Quentin's South Block. Upon arrival in your cell, people will ask to see your paperwork describing your case and charges, so they can determine whether or not you are someone with whom they want to associate. Not everyone does this, but at some point, why you are in prison will be questioned.

The SNY population is hated by General Population and Corrections Officers. Within the SNY population, sex offenders and snitches are the most hated of all. The lowest of the low are often attacked and threatened. I have had to lie and avoid making any connections with anyone in here the entire time. I don't talk much, don't go to yard, don't get too close and don't tell anyone why I'm really here. When asked, I say I'm here for a robbery, then try to change the subject as quickly as possible. I look normal enough not to raise suspicion and am not a small/vulnerable person.

I am also a sex offender sentenced to 12 years for molesting a 15-year-old girl. I am the most hated.

In a time when we are forced into isolation and serious mental stress, my situation is even more difficult to handle. In San Quentin, the bars are open and people talk through them day and night. Your neighbors want to know who you are. They want to ask why you're here and how much time you have — questions I try to avoid but I've learned that complete silence is very, very, suspicious and raises flags I don't need. So, I lie, and people accept my lies.

Am I going to die in here?

I got sick the same week the lockdown started. I had flu-like symptoms and no energy at all. I lay there hoping to live and when I found the energy, I would write to my family. We were not given any updates in the beginning, only rumors from people coming back from medical appointments saying how many people were dying and how quickly the virus was spreading. I lay there.

Am I going to die here? The most hated. Do I even deserve to live?

8/5/20

Pen name: Damian Black

Bio: 26, Born in California, I am a father, husband & a good person who made a terrible mistake.

Unique Experience / Story:

I have been in San Quentin since November 5th 201? Out of all the people here in San Quentins South block Alpine section, I am almost certain I have been here the longest out of everyone currently here. I have seen hundreds of people come & go, leaving me behind. Do to an issue regarding the counselor charge of my transfer process being reassigned, my ~~file~~ was processing was delayed. The month of March is supposed to be the month I would finally leave this rible place to the best prison in all of California that did not happen. The week I was scheduled to leave is the week transfers stopped & the beginning of our lockdown process started. Since I arrived to ison, things have always been harder for me compared to most others. Alpine section is for what's called

e are forced into isolation & serious mental stress.
/ situation is even more difficult to handle. In
Quentin the bars are open & people talk through
em day & night. Your neighbors want to know who
are. They want to ask why you're here & how much
ne you have. Questions I try to avoid but I've
rned that complete silence is very very suspicious
raises flags I don't need. So I lie. & people
ept my lies. In a time where we need all the
p we can get, I remain silent so I don't draw
attention to myself. Being locked down day after
, watching people in gowns & masks pass by day &
nt. Not knowing whether you would wake up tomorrow.
I going to die in here? I get sick the same week
lockdown started. I had flu like symptoms & had
nergy at all. I lay there hoping to live & when I
the energy I would write to my family. We were
given any updates in the beginning, only rumors from
ple coming back from medical appointments saying
many people were dying & how quickly the virus
spreading. I lay there. Am I going to die
e? The most hated. Do I even deserve to
?

Excerpt from:

¿QUÉ TENEMOS?

GENARO FERRO

¿Qué tenemos? Me pregunto cada día
Cosa hoy difícil contestar,
hay ya tanta y tanta porquería
que imposible es poderla controlar.

¿Qué tenemos? Me pregunto cada día
Y poco a poco me voy a contestar,
pues lo que antes era fantasía
hoy día lo debemos aguantar.

...

What do we have? Every day I ask myself
And it is something hard to say.
There is so much crap and shit
That failure is the only way.

What do we have? Every day I ask myself
And answers bit by bit I'm going to get.
Every nightmare from the past
Today, as normal, we must accept.

AN ENEMY UNSEEN

MICHAEL WEISE

Greg saw Southside coming, two pieces of sharp steel
duct taped to his hands, just a moment before he struck.
A moment in prison is an eternity. It's the difference
between a knife through the kidney and one sliding just
next to it. A moment is a lot of blood loss instead of a
loss of life.

Southside got five years stacked on his life sentence
and two years in AdSeg.

Greg got 37 stitches, and he got to keep breathing for
a while. Greg also saw them coming down the run, six
deep and he knew someone was about to learn a lesson.
Thank God he didn't have to see it, but he heard it, the
initial slapping of flesh, and then the weeping as they
each took their turn with him.

He will need stitches too, just in a different place.

Snitches in prison have a very short life expectancy and
being raped is better than being dead, at least some of
the time, and so [he knows] he'll have a spotty memory
about who was actually there.

Recently though, Greg heard about another type of inmate
on the unit, one a person can't fight. It is invisible but
kills you just as dead, injecting its DNA, reproducing
inside until fit to burst with its predatory offspring.
Greg tells his mama, "It'll be OK," but he means OK, like
when her grieving is over, because he is not OK.

Greg's mind flashes back to that day, April 1st. His
buddy called to see if he'd drive a truck to Dallas for

him. Greg didn't want to, but even with two jobs the ends just weren't meeting. It had been the third hour of his son crying and the fact he couldn't afford the child's Tylenol to bring his fever down that did it. He called his buddy back; it was just two kilos and it paid $1,000.

The judge sat on his bench and told him he was the worst kind of person, that he didn't care about society or the harm innocent people suffered because of these drugs. Greg told him he never intended to hurt anyone. The judge replied, "The law doesn't care about your intentions, it cares about the reality of what happens."

Greg was sentenced to ten years in prison; his lawyer said he'd be out in three, and after four parole hearings they gave him a "serve all." Three years my ass, Greg thought.

Now it's hard to breathe. There are over 7,000 confirmed cases of COVID-19 system-wide, and Greg is one of them. At the moment he is handcuffed to a hospital bed. The cold steel has rubbed a halfmoon bruise into his wrist but that is the least of his problems right now. The ventilator isn't helping much anymore, and things are getting fuzzy, blurred around the edges, like his vision when he would swim all day as a kid. Greg also feels like he has been holding his breath all day.

Maybe someone has called his mama, because he can hear her voice, frail and tinny, and he tells her that he loves her. Greg can't understand the reply but knows it's "I love you, too," and tells her, "They sentenced me to death, Mama."

WHAT HAS CHANGED?

LAILA YAGHI

They say COVID has changed so many things
What has changed for me?
My son still lies between the barren walls of a jail
In faraway chambers
Hidden between the Adirondacks
And dim lights
The many lakes that formed from prisoners' tears
The thick fog that accumulates from their sighs
Many asking why

The sun rises lazily in the morning
Between purple and blue clouds
Covering its face with its rays
Wishing the night to come early
To relieve it from witnessing
The injustices done to some innocent men

What has COVID done?
But confine him
Between more rules
More layers of darkness

The snow falls there even in June
Leaving marks of footsteps
Of innocent gazelles eaten by grizzly bears

Here at home
The sun rises or doesn't
Nothing matters
The curtains are closed
They cling tightly to the sweat of
The windows
Begging to be left alone

At night the owl moans and hoots
The crows fly away
The angels leave

Every time I pass them
I see the anger, hate and bigotry
Burning every leaf that falls from the trees
Charring the grass
And the colonies of ants

I never could understand hate
And how much it takes away from a being
Peeling away their layers of skin
Exposing their rotting, black hearts
With dark red and yellow stripes

SILVER LININGS

SEAMUS FENWAY

Through a gray, looming cloud over sorrow-filled lives,
And while broken hearts grieve for the loved lain to rest,
Silver linings shine proud, from behind faceless eyes,
With the strength to relieve all the pained and distressed.

As a torrent of doubt floods a river of tears,
And a suffering dread cripples worry-wracked minds,
Silver linings reach out, well-entrenched against fear,
And hold fast to a pledge to help man the frontline.

Amid pleas for a peace from what's taken its toll,
Among all who are trapped in a mountain of loss,
Silver linings release, from the depths of their souls,
The raw courage they've tapped in support of the cause.

See the forest, abound, for the rose-colored trees,
Each frail branch that has healed, grateful for each new day,
Silver linings beam down with compassionate ease,
And the solace revealed once the gray drifts away.

COLLECTIONS
OF
SCARS
TELL
STORIES

UNTITLED

SEAN FLATT

Splat! echoes through our cell.

I know I couldn't have stopped him. Maybe I could have put my arms out to break his fall — but I didn't even try.

I sit stunned, staring at my senseless celly. His over-weight body lies crumpled like a car crash. Blood blooms in the pool of puke. A cold sweat drips down my body; my stomach starts to quiver and I have to breathe carefully to prevent myself from puking.

I'm locked in a vomit-covered cell with a celly who's twacking out. He has fallen and is now bleeding pro-fusely. Also, I'm not seeing him breathe.

If he dies, they will automatically put me under inves-tigation and in the box — indefinitely. When they need to hold someone responsible, they will blame me. D.O.C. doesn't play fair. I panic.

"Dirty! — Hey Dirty!" I poke his leg; nothing.

Still nothing.

"Hey Dirty!" I yell. "Wake up!" I shake his leg harder.

"Dirty! — Hey Dirty! Hey Dirty!" I say louder.

I see the claws of the K-2 sinking deeper into his body. The chemicals cause his hands to clench into the mon-strous shapes of dying bugs. He bites his tongue and looks possessed.

"We need help in here!" I scream at the cell door. It doesn't respond.

I plot a path to the door. For a second I consider using Dirty as a stepping stone until I see a clean spot beside our commode/sink/kitchenette and jump over him.

I misjudge the distance. Chunky bits of barf sluice between my toes as I land. Stretching out proves to be a bigger mistake when I lose my balance and fall backwards.

Splat! My back lands. *Tunk!* My head follows.

I am now soaked in disgust and I slap my hand down to scramble out. My palm slips and I fall sideways into the sticky hell. Eye-to-eye with Dirty.

My stomach loses control and I launch a barrage of barf at Dirty. I clamber to the commode. My mouth tastes of vomit; I can't say with certainty it's all mine.

The steel door rolls open, count is clear. Prisoners pour from their cells.

"Swack! Swack!" I slap the guards' glass; their heads snap in my direction and glower at me.

"My celly fell off his rack!" They turn to the crowd at my cell.

Sarge and a trainee venture from their post.

"What happened?" the trainee asks.

"I dunno."

"He's twacking out!" Sarge yells. The trainee glares at me like I raped his regal flag.

"Move!" Sarge yells and kneels down in Dirty's muck.

"How are you doing, Ben?" the Sarge says as if soothing a sick son. I didn't know Dirty's name was Ben.

"Why do you smoke that shit?" the trainee asks.

"I don't," I say.

"Wake up, Ben!" Sarge continues to coax him. "You must, you're covered in vomit."

He makes a good point, which pisses me off. "I don't smoke that."

"Cuff him!!" Sarge cuts me off.

"Turn around."

I pause for a second, before I realize resistance is futile.

I want to scream, "I hate that crap! I see the evil it does!" I stand there humiliated and seething as the nurse comes in with a gurney.

"Twacking out?"

Sarge nods at her.

"Drag him to the hall," she says.

"What if he's paralyzed?" the trainee asks.

"He's not and that's the least of his issues. His central nervous system is shutting down." She shakes her head in frustration. She looks around at the inmates.

"Do y'all know what this junk does to you?"

"Tell them," the Sarge urges her. She hesitates.

"That junk you smoke is a nerve agent. It's sprayed with oven cleaner and bug killer, that's why he's clenching up like a dying bug."

The inmates stare at her.

The Sarge looks at her and shakes his head.

"Have y'all ever seen an oil spill?" A couple of heads begin to nod. She continues. "You've seen it when the birds and fish are covered in goo and can't breath or even clean it off themselves?" About half the heads nod.

"That's what happens to your neurons - your brain cells are all covered in a nasty chemical goo that's meant to kill bugs or weeds."

"Is he going to die?" the trainee asks.

"Who knows?" she says. "His body is trying to fight off the poison now. Hopefully his body wins."

"How many have died so far this year?" Sarge asks.

"Six, maybe seven. One is still in ICU with no brain activity," she says.

"In all of D.O.C.?" the trainee asks.

"No, just this camp," the nurse says.

The trainee stands there dumbfounded, then glares at me while I wait to go to the box.

"But y'all just keep smoking that shit and killing yourselves for all I care. Hell, that's what I get paid for!"

They load Ben on the gurney.

After the nurse leaves, Sarge and the trainee toss my cell looking for K-2 and other contraband.

My anger at Ben diminishes. I say a silent prayer for him and my own kids; I need to apologize to them, for not being there to help them, to guide them, to protect them.

When the guards are done, the young trainee chews me out. "Your cell-mate may die and you don't even give a fuck, do ya?"

"I can't stand that crap!" I shout in anger, stepping up to him. "I see what it does to those guys all the time!" Angry tears well up in my eyes. "I got kids older than you — old enough to be in here, and I worry about them all the time!" I expect them to hit me or gas me any minute now.

"Go start the paperwork," Sarge tells the trainee.

When the trainee walks away, the Sarge stares at me with steel eyes, searching my soul. I stare back, searching his.

"You don't smoke, do you?" he says.

"I hate that shit. It's evil." I wipe my face on my shoulder.

"Turn around." He uncuffs me. "That cell is a mess, I'll open the mop closet for you. Get yourself cleaned up."

He walks back to his world in the bubble as one of hundreds of dealers walks past me. "Two Dolla Holla on the market. Two Dolla Holla!"

PRISON STRUGGLES

JIMMY MURDOCK

I been pushed off hope so many times
I learned to land with no parachute.
Tell faith I don't need a Rubik's cube,
I need two wishes,
Wish one.
To have half a wish to wish on,
I'd rub that thing like a genie.
The last thing I remember dreaming was
Please let this nightmare stop.
3,741 unjustified days
but I ain't counting
I compress all my rage
Into a mountain
Then climb into the volcano.
It's hard to say when I'll lose
My sanity again so I quit looking
And stared with my eyes wide open
My mind choked up and my spirit died,
Then a wise man told me
"Sometimes the best jokes come from the worst things"
I BEEN LAUGHING MY ASS OFF SINCE.
I still hate mirrors and the ceiling is a fence,
The safest place for my mind to run wild,
Cause all these serial homicides got me petrified
I might not survive
Even in a place as laidback as Anonymous C.I.
You might get boiled alive or starved to death
Or sent back to the dorm to drop dead
Right in front of the officer's station
An inhale away from an inhaler.
But it's still safer than a trip to the panhandle
Where they lay hands on you like grandmammies
at a tent revival

The president himself endorsed the regional violence
Murder as a way to control immigration
It might have been a joke, but they treat us
like demonstrations
How many punches to the face will make a skull cave in?
How many sprays of chemical weapons will suffocate
a grown man?
Nobody knows so they just gave him the whole can.
It's not even a war, it's a million tiny massacres
The justice system laughs at us.
Like 20,000 grievances must be lying
But I seen a man's head tongue-tied to the sidewalk
He didn't even cry as the C.O. used it as a soap box
To impart this message that:
We're not important, not even human,
just imported poison to be preyed upon by eulogies.
Even with halos on, heaven's hard to find
I ran through the tunnel, dodging light like a vampire
My life's at stake here and I don't want to raise the
ire of the wrong administration
So take these pages and burn them like feathers
Cause the last stairway dropped me off at hell.
It was a long-ass ride
I'm more worn than the bus tires and twice as deflated.

I
HAVE
TO
PAY
MY
DEBT
TO
SOCIETY
BUT
I WAS
NEVER
SENTENCED
TO
DIE

Excerpt from:

HARLEM WORLD

<u>JAMES TERRY II</u>

What you staring at?

You act like you done never seen a drunk after a night off, being on a crack binge, who's been up all night and is wearing an orange jumpsuit from county jail before.

I know you rich people in the front row aren't going to let these handcuffs and shackles offend your sensibilities?

Simply exercise some patience.

Rich mother wearing a textbook stare of impotence on his face. Looking at me as if needing to kneel on my neck just to achieve a climax.

I won't permit you to George Floyd me!

Black Lives Matter!

Sitting in the front aisle in a tuxedo, with a woman so fine!! I would suck her daddy's toes just to date her.

I smell you from up here girl!

What perfume you got on, Elizabeth Taylor?

Is that stole fox or chinchilla?

Boy! Stop sipping whilst I'm talking. These people paid good money to get inside this theatre to be entertained. Social distancing aside.

Give the lady the rest of that bottle!

Hey! Girl! What's your name?

Serendipity!!

How the hell you spell that??

S...A...R...in... You sure your parents not Black folks
and you just passing for White?

Alright, let me leave you good Caucasians alone. Please
save your applause for a more poignant point in time of
tonight's performance.

Welcome to The Apollo Theatre!

I'll be giving you a one-man act tonight that is an
exclusive, never to be repeated.

When this gig was first presented to my estate trustees,
they were hesitant to take on such a proficient script.
The talent pool originally approached was admirable,
yet they were also afraid to support an unknown Black
imprisoned author.

This being his first foray into late night comedy.
Can't you see me entertaining these fine people?

Yeah! Yeah! I get it Serendipity!

She done downed the whole bottle. Now, as a housewife of New York, she about to get real due to intoxication. She wants to come up with her own show as heckler and have an eloquent epilogue.

Shows like this cost money!

It's time to hold church in here.

Sell him a Honda, sell him a Honda! Subaru Ferrari, Subaru Ferrari!!

Good God! Caught in the Holy Ghost and started talking in tongues.

I'm a hologram! You're right once again Serendipity! I'm transparent and shallow. You can see right through me!

Well! I hope you've enjoyed yourselves and my performance.

I'm a Virtual Reality Richard Pryor, a runaway slave, because these trustees still going to the bank making a killing off my deceased Black behind.

To all Abolitionists, Conductors, and Harriet Tubman the original Black Unicorn (shout out to Tiffany Haddish).

Thanks to your efforts with The Underground Railroad... That when I left...it was on The Elevated Train!

Black Lives Matter! Aspiring Black literary artists can even be found in the frozen tundra of the most rural Wisconsin penal system.

Seek and you shall find oppressed voices reaching out to be heard.

OR GIVE ME...

JOSHUA L. WELLS

Give me Liberty or give me...

Purpose presupposes fortitude, internal grit
In face of indefatigable odds or international insanity.
Humanity's questions of loss
Weighed against loss of humanity. Look me in the eye
And tell me Freedom's worth.
Because panic precipitates slavery, slavish worship
Before idols of security, statistics, and another model
Fraught with flaws. Pandemic laws
Poured from on high, infodemic edicts from lying lips.
Public masters our new gods.
In experts we trust.
Not how life used to be. Remember when...

Give me Liberty or give me...

Patriots are dying breeds. Soft couches
And cushioned living have ways of erasing memories,
Momentary madness creating amnesia
Whilst erstwhile kings and self-appointed deities
Sip honey-crushed ambrosia from clasped golden cups,
Heedless to the men they're crushing.
Government is everything. All others
Just subjects in inconvenient sentences
Who need their statements cut short, period.
Questions dared are only marks, headaches
To be dealt poisoned pills.
That'll fix 'em! Remember when...

Give me Liberty or give me...

But that was back when terms like Tyranny
Held heart-chilling meaning. Preaching peacocks

Who held up virtue-signaled plumage
Were not to be tolerated. Speak plain.
Speak clear. Speak truth. The first of three,
Life, was useless without Liberty, promise founded
On Happiness rightly pursued. Now listen to the
nightly newsmen.
Preening, self-congratulatory views pounded
The peasant-class plebs bite another bullet,
Inhale bullplop by the plateful
Then, grateful, beg for more. Remember when
imposed servitude
Spelled grounds for war? But now we scrape,
Content to wallow in indifference, bow in deference
To our elitist betters, become willing wimps suckling
from Netflix pacifiers and Twitter feeds.

Because someone else can meet my needs,
just so Alexa's close at hand. Hey, Alexa,
Can you replay some history? Remember when...

Give me Liberty or give me...

Death.

AN ANT'S LIFE

JUSTIN SLAVINSKI

There's a fan at the foot of my bunk. One of those industrial oscillating deals that belongs in a warehouse. It's
mounted on the wall and drones on day after day, hour
after hour, resting each morning for the ten minutes it
takes to sweep and mop the area I live in. After that:
hummmmm; the fan whirrs back to life and resumes its
endless mission to relieve the oppressive heat in here.

I've been quarantined with 63 others in a large room
for the past four months. Imagine living in a house
with no internal walls where 63 other people also live.
Sure, at times this could be seen as a blessing. While
people in the free world came up with creative ways to
entertain themselves or to avoid their spouses (see:
wine sales have spiked nationwide), things never got
old or boring in here.

But if you thought your brother, dad, spouse, child,
cousin, nephew, or dog got on your nerves, imagine 63
of them. Imagine 64 men in a 3,500-square foot space as
spring became summer in South Florida. Imagine the heat.
Oh, and there's no air-conditioning. Warehousing already
causes stress to run high like a COVID-19 fever; compound
that stress with no programs, no canteen, and no recreation — the three life-sustaining activities for most
incarcerated individuals — and our stress is a pot on a
stove boiling over.

Beneath the fan is my footlocker, which holds most of
the possessions I've accumulated in prison. Sure, since
the crisis began I've had a mesh bag full of junk food
hanging from my bunk for emergency rations. But most
of what my locker holds is not food or condiments, not

honeybuns or off-brand coffee. It's paper. There are
reading selections from writing classes I've taken, a few
quality examples of my own writing, four-year-old articles from *New York Times Magazine* I've saved for some
reason obvious only to the Justin from the past, eight
pressed four-leaf clovers, certificates I've earned, pho-
tos of my family, scraps of letters and sentiment from
years ago. It's a history of my time spent doing right
and being productive.

Near my locker — and sometimes beside, around, beneath,
or simply crawling up the side — are ants. The ants —
like me — have lost interest in the usual things they
should care about, like sugar, candy, or sweets. I have
dozens of sugar packets in my locker, a few bags of
overpriced chocolate chip cookies, and the odd ketchup
packet that was not QCed at the factory and has oozed
high fructose corn syrup from its crimped top or bottom.
The ants have no interest in my sugar. Instead they're
interested in my sweat-soaked, day-old laundry which
rests beside my locker on the floor in another mesh bag.

We are in Florida, and what cools our living space
the most is not night time, but rain. When rain falls
briefly during the day and the sun returns, our nights
are miserable, tossing-and-turning affairs. When rain
visits late and the sun is obscured until it slips
below the horizon, our nights are pleasant enough for
sound sleep. Then, however, the mayflies (or whatever
they are) show up. Utterly harmless, probably incapable
of eating or biting, seeking only to reproduce, they
flit around, orbiting the dorm's fluorescent lights in
wonky elliptical orbits. When a kindly overseer turns
off half the lights the mayflies don't join up with
their potential mates at other lights. Instead, they
find their way to the oscillating fan above my bed,
where they're decapitated in droves. My bed becomes
their graveyard.

Do insects think about purpose? Do they try to find meaning in the midst of a crisis? Do they go through bouts of depression, wallowing and wandering, eating out of boredom, watching far too much T.V., and forget to shave every day? Do the ants that creep in under the emergency door by my bunk to crawl all over my dirty laundry worry they haven't written anything meaningful in over a month? Do the amorous mayflies that lose their lives to the whirling blades of death above my bed care that there's no end in sight for this prolonged quarantine?

I doubt it. For all my complaints about insects, I do admire their single-minded resolve to complete goals, whatever they might be — even if their pursuit ends in death. They want food; they spread out and seek it. They want love; they buzz around until they find it. They want a cooler home; they build or sacrifice to achieve it. Sure, most are focused on food or survival, but so am I. Deep down, I know there's more to life than survival — even in this place, even at this time.

This is where my mind goes while I stare at the fan above my bunk. I should be working out or reading a book or writing my family more often, or shaving or planning a D&D campaign. But I'm not and I don't and I haven't.

Maybe I need to be more like the insects. Maybe I need to be more like the fan — single-minded and only turning off for ten minutes each day.

This is where I am right now: sweeping up ant and mayfly corpses by my bunk, pondering whether or not I could achieve something if I poured myself into it with single-minded intensity. But I just don't think I can.

INDEX

A

B

I'm the oldest of four and John was the second. I was born in Hamilton, Ohio and grew up mostly in Ohio but lived in both Michigan and Florida as a child and Ohio and Florida as an adult. We moved to FL when I was 17. I went to school in Gainesville, John went to the Army and I eventually went back to Ohio as well. Then he moved to FL, all Hell broke loose and we all tried to come back to be close to him but that never worked out.

I was a Firefighter/Paramedic before going back to college at Miami University of Ohio, got a BA and MA in Philosophy and a JD from University of Cincinnati College of Law. I have been practicing mostly Family law for over 16 years and some criminal defense work as a public defender in the city where I live. I had a daughter who took her own life four years ago at 27. I had to tell my brother over the phone and hope he'd be ok. He loved her too.

But, I am happy with "John's sister."

BECKER, DAVE

Throw Away the Keys Please

pg. 049

–

I don't usually get into writing much, but these are special times. Thank you for giving us inmates a voice.

. . .

Incarcerated in:
The State of Florida

BLACK, DAMIAN

Untitled – pg. 166

–

26, Born in California. I am a father, husband, and a good person who made a terrible mistake. I hope my story leaves the reader needing to take a deep breath. I take one every day.

The message I really want to convey is just how hated sex offenders are. How I have almost no one to trust or befriend. How isolation on top of isolation is driving me crazy. At night, someone yells good night to everyone and at the end, says, "And to all those not celled up with a sex offender tonight, "GOODNIGHT!!! Kill yourself, you piece of shit! Swallow a razor blade! Jump off the 5th tier!"

Every night.

I would also like to say that I am [self-proclaimed] innocent of the charge that carries the most time and makes my case violent. I kissed her. I never should have done that. I deserve to be here.

Incarcerated in:
The State of California

B

BOUDICCA

Ticket to Ride — pg. 043

—

Boudicca is an incarcerated writer. She appears frequently as a guest blogger on *Adventures in Camp Prisoney Land* and in 2017 won a PEN America award for poetry. Her work is also published in *Scalawag Magazine* and *Cream City Review*.

She plays the dulcimer and the piano.

...

Incarcerated in:
The State of Florida

BREHMER, DENALI

Locks and Keys — pg. 160

—

I like to write a lot. It's my passion, hobby, and I guess I'm good at it. I've been incarcerated for a little over a year now and am looking at serious time. I work any job so I can keep busy and I get to exercise. I love the color purple and my favorite dog breeds are rottweilers and mutts. Yes, I am 20 years old and it shows a lot, but I still feel older than my 90-year old grandmother. I hope you like my piece.

...

Incarcerated in:
The State of Alaska

C

CASERES, LESMES

The Shakedown — pg. 016
—

Lesmes is a writer serving
a 25-year prison sentence in
FDOC. His writing has been
published by Exchange for
Change and duendeliterary.org.
To see a reading of his work,
go to YouTube and search for,
"Voices from the Inside."

Mr. Caseres hopes to publish
his prison memoir upon his
release, scheduled for 2026.

...

Incarcerated in:
The State of Florida

D

DALY, CORAL

Excerpt from "Mirroring a
Mask" — pg. 154
—

My name is Coral Daly. Some
say that I am young at heart
with an old soul. I'm 46 years
old. I have a handsome 17-year-
old son named D'Artagnan.

I have a passion-filled heart
for writing, that's what makes
me tick. I still prefer pen
and paper to typing on a com-
puter. Words flow through me
like currents in tides. I also
enjoy outdoor activities such
as camping, fishing, kayaking
and riding my motorcycle. I
live in Anchorage, Alaska. I
plan on traveling cross country on my motorcycle, solo.

...

Incarcerated in:
The State of Alaska

D

DEMERS, LAWRENCE

I Can't Breathe – pg. 134
–

Incarcerated in:
The State of Florida

DeMORETA, EDWARD

COVID-19 vs. the Mountain
pg. 068
–

Edward DeMoreta is a graduate
of Southeastern University, a
former geometry teacher, and a
father of three.

While incarcerated, he redis-
covered a passion for writing
through the Exchange for
Change program and uses it
as a creative and therapeutic
outlet.

He considers himself a movie
buff and enjoys pizza more than
any other food, but has yet to
find a pizza place that deliv-
ers to prisons. His goal is to
find joy within each day.

. . .

Incarcerated in:
The State of Florida

F

FENWAY, SEAMUS

Silver Linings — pg. 175
—

My name is Seamus Fenway (only
one person in the world will
grasp the significance of this
pen name and I hope it makes
her laugh).

I've just passed the halfway
mark of my sentence, having
served five years of a ten-
year sentence. In 2017, I sat
at a table in our crowded
chow hall eating a relatively
traditional Thanksgiving meal,
causing me to reflect on
where I was, why I was here,
and who I was missing at this
time of the year.

Nearly five years later, that
reflection has spawned about
100 poems, from introspective
to the funny, from the sad
to the celebratory. It is my
wish that once I have rejoined
society, I am able to publish
some or all of the poetry I
write, along with my ten years
of journal entries, into a
book that inspires others.

...

Incarcerated in:
The State of Virginia

FERNANDEZ, EMILIO C.

Broken Tiles — pg. 106
—

This piece was written in
response to hearing that my
best friend Joe had passed
away on July 15, 2020, due to
complications from COVID-19.

...

Incarcerated in:
The State of Florida

F

FERRO, GENARO

Excerpt from "¿Qué Tenemos?"
pg. 170
—

Genaro Ferro, Cuban, is currently imprisoned at Everglades
Correctional Institution. In
his spare time he writes essays
and poems about the fragments
of the world that reach him.
He is divorced and a father of
three.

...

Genaro Ferro, Cubano, actual-
mente encarcelado en la prisión
de Everglades Correctional
Institution. En sus ratos
libres escribe ensayos y poe-
mas plasmando en ellos lo que
ve des mundo actual. el es
divorciado y padre de tres
hijos.

...

Incarcerated in:
The State of Florida

FINLEY, ERIC

Bullseye — pg. 069
—

I am 55 years old and I write
daily. I am working on the
last chapter of my third
novel. In less than two years
I will be released and I am
going to become a full-time
writer. It will be a career
change made late in life yet I
am confident I will find it to
be more enjoyable and professional than crime and prison.

...

Incarcerated in:
The State of Florida

G

FLATT, SEAN

Untitled — pg. 178

—

My name is Sean Flatt.

In 2016 I came to Florida,
with my family on vacation —
I caught 35 years. I was 50
years old and had never been to
prison.

Before I came to prison I was a
successful electrician for over
25 years and always promised my
kids I would be there for them
— to protect — to help them.

I am now retooling my brain to
become a writer. Hopefully I
can become successful enough to
help my kids through college.

I promised I would always help
and take care of them. I intend
to fulfill my promise and obli-
gation even here - in prison.

I hope you appreciate
this story.

...

Incarcerated in:
The State of Florida

GARCIA, JOE

The Hearts, Minds and
Stomachs of Grown-Ass Men
pg. 071

—

Joe Garcia is incarcerated at
San Quentin State Prison where
he is a staff member of the *San
Quentin News* newspaper and *Wall
City* magazine.

He is an editorial associate for the Prison Journalism
Project and has been published
in the *Sacramento Bee* and the
Washington Post.

...

Incarcerated in:
The State of California

→

G

GOMEZ, VICTOR

I Wish I Could During COVID-19 — pg. 031

—

Victor Gomez is Associate Deputy Warden in the Arizona Department of Corrections

GUERRA, GUSTAVO

The New Normal — pg. 099

—

Gustavo Guerrra is currently serving a natural life sentence in the Florida Department of Corrections.

He discovered a passion for writing as a result of particating in the volunteer-led Exchange for Change program.

Other essays by him can be found in *Don't Shake the Spoon, Vol. 2*, and on the <u>drunkenodyssey.com</u>. He can usually be found writing, complaining about the heat, or playing a ninth level rogue in his D and D campaign.

. . .

Incarcerated in: The State of Florida

H

HILL, JOHNNY LEE

We are the Same — pg. 114
—

My name is Johnny Lee Hill,
incarcerated in Florida with
a 15-year minimum mandatory
sentence (I am currently seven
years into my sentence and have
eight years left).

I am also a visually-impaired/
legally blind individual who
LOVES books. I wasn't born
with my impairment, though. It
occurred in 2016, while still
in prison, from an attempted
suicide.

Being in prison and solitary
confinement (where I was at the
time) had made me so depressed
that I just wanted to "end it
all." Instead of losing my life,
I lost most of my vision. But,
I haven't lost my LOVE of writing and bringing words to life
on paper.

Although I have a disability,
I DO NOT consider myself as
a "disabled." So, I strive to
still be a writer.

...

Incarcerated in:
The State of Florida

K

KELLEY, NIGEL

Untitled — pg. 146
—

Nigel, 41, is a seventh generation Floridian and father with
a love for the outdoors and a
zest for growing his own food
forest one day.

When he's not mentoring others
or working on his own personal
growth, he is a zealous reader,
writer and thinker.

Nigel aspires to live a self-
sustainable abundant life upon
his release from prison and
continue to spiritually mentor
others that are still behind
the walls.

...

Incarcerated in:
The State of Florida

K

KELLY, KEVIN F.

artwork — pg. 139

—

Incarcerated in:
The State of California

KING, SAMUEL M.

Pandemic — pg. 036

—

I appreciate the opportunity
to submit these poems as an
incarcerated writer as we too-
often are ignored and rendered
voiceless.

My awareness of issues and
current events comes from a
long history and experiences
as an African American male;
i.e. struggle of racism - Equal
Rights Movement, violence,
mass incarceration, Jim Crow
— ancestors who were slaves
— generations of sharecrop-
pers. As well as being a Baby
Boomer and Vietnam-era Veteran
— drafter 1968.

My style of poetry is "rant-
ing" which is different from
mainstream American poetry or
rapping — I have several chap-
books of rants. Thank you for
the opportunity to share my
style, thoughts, and rants with
you. I am Sam I am.

...

Incarcerated in:
The State of Utah

L

M

LIVINGSTON, JOSEPH

Journey Through COVID

pg. 090

–

Joseph Livingston is 63 years old, a citizen of the U.S. Virgin Islands, presently incarcerated at Everglades Correctional Institution.

Previously published articles include several in the *Everglades Endeavor*. He enjoys writing, reading, listening to a variety of music, and regularly exercising to stay mentally and physically fit.

. . .

Incarcerated in:
The State of Florida

MAC, BIG

Gone Too Soon – pg. 124

–

Incarcerated in:
The State of Florida

M

MALEC, CHRISTOPHER

Am I Speaking Hebrew?

pg. 119

—

Born and raised in Hollywood, Florida, Christopher Malec has served nearly 12 years of the Life Without Parole sentence he was given at 19. Through his time as an inmate law clerk, he discovered a love for law, philosophy, and writing.

As a poet, he seeks to illuminate the lives of the incarcerated and the injustices those behind the fences of prisons experience. As a way of activism, his writing works to indict the justice system at large and bring it to trial. He is 31 years old, and in January of 2021, was named the Luis Hernandez Prison Poet Laureate by two South Florida nonprofits: Exchange for Change and O, Miami.

...

Incarcerated in:
The State of Florida

MARTIN III, BILLY F.

Dissident — pg. 158

—

A little about me...well; I've been through hell...I turned 40, March 8, 2020, And I am on a "B" letter with a 15-year mandatory P.R.R. sentence. Actually, it is two fifteens and two fives...but they are concurrent, so who's counting, right?

I have been on the street a total of one year since April 1, 2005...And seven and a half months of that was in 2006. I was out 38 days in 2011 and three and a half months in 2017. My current T.R.D. is January 28, 2033...and, yes, apparently...I like it here.

I have a history that quite easily could have ended me some life sentences...I am very grateful that I have a date at all...I have barely managed to stay alive 40 years.

...

Incarcerated in:
The State of Florida

MARTINEZ, EDUARDO

COVID Crazy — pg. 017

—

Eduardo "Echo" Martinez
was born in Miami in 1979. He
was raised in Carol City and
has been writing most of his
life. He has a 22-year-old son
and his muse is his wife, for
whom he waited 16 years to
marry.

His work has appeared in
anthologies, *Cuban Counter-
points*, *Scalawag* and *Don't
Shake the Spoon: A Prison
Writing Journal*.

A chapbook of his poetry is
forthcoming. His poetry has
been heard on PBS, NPR, and
he was featured on his local
CBS station. He was the Luis
Hernandez Prison Poet Laureate from 1/2019 through
1/2021.

...

Incarcerated in:
The State of Florida

MARTINEZ, ISRAEL (IZZY)

Untitled — pg. 113

—

Israel Martinez was born in
1988 in North Carolina but has
lived in Miami since he was
six. Early on he began writing
short stories favoring charac-
ters akin to Batman and Knight
Rider. He then went on to con-
ceptualize his ideas into an
art form and became enamored by
the medium.

When he was sentenced in 2013
he continued writing until his
heart bled onto the pages. He
has been published in two edi-
tions of Exchange for Change's
literary journal: *Don't Shake
the Spoon*, and his poetry was
featured in the Miami Herald.

He recently learned to play
guitar and sing, and joined
a band before becoming its
leader. He is due to be
released in 10/25, when he has
aspirations to continue writing and inform the world of the
malpractices of Florida's criminal justice system.

...

Incarcerated in:
The State of Florida

M

MONN, TRAVIS R.

My Escape — pg. 156

—

I am 38 years old. I was
born on 7-26-1982 in Yakimo,
Washington and am currently
serving a 122-year sentence in
San Quentin State Prison for
armed robbery.

. . .

Incarcerated in:
The State of California

MOORE, KEVIN M.

artwork — front cover

—

Incarcerated in:
The State of Florida

MOSER, RYAN M.

*I Can't Stand Talking About
the Coronavirus, and Other
Complaints — pg. 057*
—

Ryan M. Moser is a recovering
addict from Philadelphia serving eight years in the Florida
DOC for property crimes.

Previous publications include
*Mississippi Quarterly,
Upstreet Literary Magazine,
December, Muse Literary
Journal, Evening Street
Press, Storyteller, Santa Fe
Literary Review, Iconoclast,
Progressive,* thewildword.
com, themarshallproject.org,
medium.com and more.

Received an Honorable Mention
for Essay from PEN American
in 2020. Nominated for Best of
the Net 2020-nonfiction and
for the Pushcart Prize 2020
nonfiction.

Ryan enjoys yoga, martial
arts, chess and has two beautiful boys.

...

*Incarcerated in:
The State of Florida*

MURDOCK, JIMMY

Prison Struggles — pg. 184
—

*Incarcerated in:
The State of Florida*

M

MURPHY, ANTOINE J.

Black Magic — pg. 135

—

Went from "actin' White" to "actin' Black."

From green cap & gown to prison greens, which I have been donning for the last 23 years. Wanted to die at first but God found me (smile). Now I consistently try to live the "abundant life" promised me.

I hope to be released by year's end & make the most of it. Fashion is in my future; so, too, songwriting & self-publishing books. My today's tomorrows will also feature "visiting those in prison."

More of my voice can be found at http://betweenthebars.org/blogs/545/.

...

Incarcerated in:
The State of Wisconsin

O

OVERTURF, HOWARD

The Murder of George Floyd
pg. 138

—

I received a 10-year sentence for a home invasion robbery; I am ashamed of my actions. I'm 40 years old and have two boys and three girls, eight to 27 years old. Prison saved my life because my addiction would have been the death of me. Since I've been in prison, I have completed the California State University Sacramento Wastewater Course and will be taking the Florida State Exam in February of 2021. I have completed the Criminon course "The Way to Happiness" and have received certificates for Anger Management, Parenting, Victim Impact, Business Concepts, Self Government, Personal Growth, Personal Finance, Microsoft Excel, Word, and Windows.

Once released I plan to mentor adolescent children. I believe it is never too late to turn your life around. Some of the best people I've met in prison are doing a life sentence.

...

Incarcerated in:
The State of Florida

P

PALERMO, LANCE E.

Social Deprivation
pg. 096

—

Lance E. Palermo is a firm
believer that higher education saved his life. By setting
goals and achieving them he
has graduated from Lee College,
Catholic Distance University
and is currently working
towards an M.B.A. through Adams
State University.

He gives all the credit and
assures none of these things
could have been possible
without God's grace and a
loving family.

...

Incarcerated in:
The State of Texas

PARKER, LEONARD L.

Excerpt from "The Worst of
Both Worlds" – pg. 131

—

My name is Leonard Parker.
I'm from Milwaukee, WI. I've
been incarcerated for almost
16 years come October. During
my incarceration I've basically bettered the best parts
of myself and destroyed the
unattractive parts that make
a person think in the ways of
foolish children or old fools.

...

Incarcerated in:
The State of Wisconsin

P

PAYNE, HELENA L.

I Can't Breathe — pg. 112

—

Incarcerated in:
The State of California

PINSEN, PIERRE

A Breathing Tribute
pg. 118

—

Pierre Pinson is a poet, author and activist [self-proclaimed] wrongfully convicted of an armed assault on a police station. Pierre is incarcerated at the Pennsylvania State correctional Institution at Fayette and would like to give reverence to all revolutionaries who have organized community and have weaponized their voices.

Hetepu.

. . .

Incarcerated in:
The State of Florida

R

PRIDE, CORY

On the Inside Looking Out
pg. 104

–

My Name is Cory Pride and I
am an emerging scholar in the
Washington University Prison
Education Program with a natural science and mathematics
concentration. My pastimes are
playing chess, dominoes, and
grueling cardio workouts to
let me know I'm alive.

. . .

Incarcerated in:
The State of Missouri

REED, MAURICE

Black is Beautiful – pg. 138
–

For the past eight years
Maurice Dupree Reed, aka Reese,
has dedicated most of his time
working on transformation and
helping others do the same by
facilitating a crime and violence prevention program – No
More Tears.

Born in CA in 1985, he is ten
years into a 15-year sentence
at San Quentin. He has partic-
ipated in numerous self-help
and therapeutic workshops, is
a college student at Patten
College, and was the headliner
music performer in SQSP, the
first ever TedX. He performed
more than 10 plays as a member of the Martin Shakespeare
Company and interned for FIRST
WATCH, a group dedicated to
humanizing incarcerated men.
Hobbies include chess, exercising, reading, writing poetry,
plays, music.

. . .

Incarcerated in:
The State of California

R

RETH, TIBNI

Blind Sestinas are Invisible in the Dictionary – pg. 052

–

Tibni Reth is currently serving a 36-year sentence for second-degree murder in the state of Alaska.

She was born in Bandung, Indonesia 57 years ago and became a naturalized citizen at the age of 12. She grew up in Southern California and graduated from Loma Linda University in California as well as from Aurora University in Illinois.

Before coming to prison, she worked in health care, social work, commercial fishing, commercial driving and aviation. Among her many hobbies are cooking and travel having visited four continents and eight countries. As of this writing, she still doesn't know what to do when she grows up.

. . .

Incarcerated in:
The State of Alaska

RICHARDSON, RODERICK

COVID-19 – pg. 086

–

I was born and raised in Miami Dade County and I've been incarcerated for over 29 years. I attended the public school system in Dade County and I realized many, many years ago that the wrong things I did to provide for my family, I could have made more positive decisions with patience and my belief in God.

Currently, I'm incarcerated at Dade CI in Homestead, FL. I'm hoping that you can relate to my COVID-19 piece. Thank you. God bless you and continue to stay positive and safe.

. . .

Incarcerated in:
The State of Florida

RIVERA, ZAZA

Excerpt from "Can't Breathe"
pg. 139
–

Zaza Rivera is an Afro-Puerto
Rican writen/spoken word artist
who is currently incarcerated
in the State of Florida.

His passion to write has led
to expressing thoughts in civil
matters such as the Black Lives
Matter movement, immigration,
mass incarceration, and the
struggles Black and Latino
families go through on a day-
by-day basis. Zaza plans to
pursue writing and performance
poetry upon his release.

...

Incarcerated in:
The State of Florida

ROGER, JOLLY

Sick – pg. 077
–

Jolly Roger is currently being
[self-proclaimed] held captive
in one of Florida's numerous
corrections facilities where
she struggles daily to main-
tain her identity and sanity.

She is kept alive by her steady
diet of hope and sarcasm and
the support of her family and
the many friends who have sur-
vived their captivity.

...

Incarcerated in:
The State of Florida

S

SLAVINSKI, JUSTIN

An Ant's Life — pg. 193

—

Justin Slavinski began his professional career as an editor and discovered the joys of writing while incarcerated through the Exchange for Change program.

His previous writing credits include: *The Everglades Endeavor, Don't Shake the Spoon Vol 2* and *Iconoclast.*

Justin enjoys teaching Intro to Writing classes, eviscerating prison cuisine through satire, accidentally eliminating all his players while GMing D&D games and eating Nutella. He currently lives in Miami.

. . .

Incarcerated in:
The State of Florida

SMITH, GLENN

Florida Set to Reduce State Prison Population by COVID-19 Deaths — pg. 080

—

Glenn Smith has been a [self-proclaimed] slave in the FDC for almost 30 years and regularly [illegible] against for filing grievances and litigation to correct wrongs and for positive change.

. . .

Incarcerated in:
The State of Florida

SMITH, WILLIAM

artwork — back cover

—

Incarcerated in:
The State of Florida

SOTO, JAMES

Who's Next? — pg. 034

—

James Soto is an incarcerated writer in the Illinois
Department of Corrections.

He is a student in the
Northwestern Prison Education
Program. He is from the
Southwest Side of Chicago.

He likes creative writing
because it pushes him to get
outside his comfort zone and
he enjoys the challenge.

...

Incarcerated in:
The State of Illinois

S

STUHLMILLER, NAVIGATOR

artwork — pg. 079

—

Previously in a Florida jail

T

TERRY II, JAMES

Excerpt from "Harlem World"
pg. 188

—

French/American citizen raised in a USAF military household in France, Germany and U.S.A. Victimized by "Karen" hoax in Madison, WI in 1990.

Past 22 years [self-proclaimed] erroneously imprisoned to a 35-year miscarriage of justice. This is second anthology I've published in and first for Harlem World. Google search "Justice for James Terry" read more science fiction, true crime novel, poems and join our fight for racial quality, truth, justice and my freedom.

. . .

Incarcerated in:
The State of Wisconsin

TORRES, GERVASIO

The Broken Home Syndrome

pg. 055

—

Gervasio Torres is a native of
South Florida.

His passion for writing has
provided a vehicle for dealing with life's challenges. His
inspiration can be found as
close as opening his mind and
as far reaching as the depths
of his imagination.

He is a member of Exchange for
Change's Leadership Council,
creator and co-facilitator for
the "Just Write" writing class
for colleagues, an active
member of the Draft Pick's
Gavel Club, and a copy editor/
senior writer for a monthly
newsletter.

. . .

Incarcerated in:
The State of Florida

TYLER, ARTHUR

artwork — pg. 227

—

Incarcerated in:
The State of Florida

WARD,
MS. ALISHA MICHELLE
Untitled — pg. 140

—

Hello! My name is Alisha Michelle Ward. I am a 49-year-old Christian transgender woman. I have lived the last 28+ in Florida prisons. I have been serving a life sentence since 1992.

While incarcerated I have completed my Masters Degree in Theology and earned various educational and vocational certifications. I have been actively facilitating and mentoring in several cognitive behavioral groups and write music. I am one of those people born with music in their soul.

...

Incarcerated in:
The State of Florida

WEISE, MICHAEL
An Enemy Unseen — pg. 171

—

My name is Michael John Weise and I am a prisoner of the Texas Department of Criminal Justice. I have been incarcerated for 11 years and am serving a 30-year prison sentence. I will be eligible for parole in February of 2024.

After coming to prison I sat down and began writing. I have now penned a series of novellas for my children named *The Chronicles of Seraphi*. The first two novellas, "Ann's Battle" (2017) and "Courtney's Choice" (2020), were self-published on Amazon CreateSpace. I have also published work in *The Old Red Kimono Magazine*, the *Willow Review*, and the online poetry journal *Ekphrastic Review*.

...

Incarcerated in:
The State of Texas

W

WELLS, JOSHUA L.

Or Give Me... – pg. 191

–

Incarcerated in:
The State of Wisconsin

WILLIAMS, BOB R. (COWBOY)

In Memoriam: 2020's COVID-19 Losses to the Death Row Community – pg. 062

–

I am Bob R. Williams, Jr., an inmate on California's vast Eath-Bound Purgatory that is Death Row. Arrested at 18, I pled guilty at 20 and have been here ever since.

I am now 44. I write, read vast amounts, and paint, as well as practice and teach yoga. Hopefully one day I will get the opportunity to work with troubled teens stuck in the juvenile system. Teens like I used to be, who have suffered the traumas of abuse and neglect, who have found themselves on the wrong side of a courtroom, all in an effort to help them find them-selves and a better way in the world that keeps them out of the pipeline to prison.

. . .

Incarcerated in:
The State of California

WILLINGHAM, ANGELA

Who CARES — pg. 155

—

Incarcerated in:
Florida Federal Prison

WRIGHT, AARON "A.J."

Excerpt from "I Will
Breathe" — pg. 141

—

Incarcerated in:
The State of Florida

X

XERXES

Untitled — pg. 040

—

XerXes grew up in Chicago and resided in Michigan a couple years prior to his offense. He has been incarcerated since 1993. He is currently a senior in an off-site liberal arts Bachelor Degree program — majoring in Ministry Leadership — with a minor in Social Work.

XerXes is a Rhetoric Center Consultant, Criminal Justice Reform advocate and an advocate of Restorative Justice. He is a member of the National Lifers of America, Inc., where he served as Chapter President from 2017-2018.

...

Incarcerated in:
The State of Michigan

Y

YAGHI, LAILA

What Has Changed? — pg. 173

—

My name is Laila Yaghi and I am the mother of an incarcerated son, Ziyad Yaghi, who is in Ray Brook, NY. He was sentenced to 31.5 years for taking an innocent trip overseas. He wanted to get to know his father's side of the family [who] reside in Jordan. The government misinterpreted everything. [I believe Ziyad] has been falsely accused. I have been trying to bring awareness to this injustice.

I was born in Montana and now am residing in NC.

PATRICK W. BERRY

is an associate professor
of writing and rhetoric at
Syracuse University. His most
recent book is *Doing Time,
Writing Lives: Refiguring
Literacy and Higher Education
in Prison* (Southern Illinois
University Press).

SOMAN CHAINANI

is a graduate of Harvard
University and Columbia
University's MFA Film Program.
Soman began his career as
a screenwriter and direc-
tor, with his films playing at
over 150 film festivals worldwide. He has been nominated
for the Waterstone Prize for
Children's Literature, named to
the Out100, and received the
$100,000 Shasha Grant and the
Sun Valley Writer's Fellowship,
both for debut writers.

His newest book, BEASTS &
BEAUTY, will be released from
Harper Collins in September
2021 and his debut series,
THE SCHOOL FOR GOOD AND EVIL,
which has sold more than three
million copies and been trans-
lated into 30 languages, will
be a NETFLIX major motion
picture in 2022.

EDWIDGE DANTICAT

is a writer living in Miami and
is a member of the Advisory
Board of Exchange for Change.

DIANE GOODMAN

is the author of three short
story collections ("Party
Girls" from Autumn House Press;
"The Plated Heart" and "The
Genius of Hunger," both from
Carnegie Mellon University
Press—Series in Short Fiction)
and various other publica-
tions, most recently *Lunches
with Louie* in "Flash Nonfiction
Food" (Woodhall Press, 2020)
and *Bluffing* ("SkyIsland
Journal" Fall 2020). She is a
professor in Phoenix, AZ.

THANK YOU

Hear Us was intended to document a moment in time. We
wanted to capture what was happening inside prisons
before the pandemic passed and life returned to normal.
Little did we know! From the 180 entries from 16 states
we selected 58 pieces from ten states.

At the time of this printing, COVID-19 continues to
spread inside our state and federal prisons. Some institutions are on their third or fourth quarantine. While
some states released people for a variety of reasons —
political and otherwise — other states remained stead-
fast in their enforcement of completing full sentences.
Edwin Lugo, housed in a Florida correctional facility
when he sent us his piece for this publication, passed
away from COVID-19 just a few years short of his ten-year
sentence. Vaccine availability for the nearly 1.3 million
people locked in state prisons is as varied as state
sentencing laws.

This book was the product of an extraordinary team
effort. Exchange for Change and Disorder Press want to
thank the editorial board that guided the initial selec-
tion process: Patrick Berry, Soman Chainani, Edwidge
Danticat and Diane Goodman, who set us on the right path
for our final selections. Thank you to our initial readers: Jill Berke, Sonesh Chainani, Meena Jagganath, Shara
Kobetz Pelz and Skylar Thompson, and to Rob Kaniuk and
Elyse Mason for their careful reading of the final product. A shoutout to our interns who helped track and tran-
scribe the hand-written submissions: Ana Sofia Garcia,
Ally Jenson and Rose Johnson. A debt of gratitude to
Jody Lewen and Michael Bien for introducing Exchange
for Change and Disorder Press to each other. Thank you,

Michelle Nazzal, for taking the contents of the book and making it into a work of art. And a particular bucket of gratitude to Lisa Palley, who volunteered countless hours to help with promotion and publicity.

On behalf of all the incarcerated writers included in this collection, and the hundreds of thousands whose words are still behind bars, we hope that you Hear Us.

KATHIE KLARREICH
Founder & Executive Director
Exchange for Change

MIKAELA GRANTHAM
Disorder Press

JOSEPH GRANTHAM
Disorder Press

E4C